ALL TUNISIA

Text by: Mrs Alia Ben Younes, Archaeologist.
Mr Habib Ben Younes, Archaeologist.

Photographs, lay-out and reproduction, entirely designed and created by the technical deparment of EDITO-
RIAL ESCUDO DE ORO, S.A.

1st Edition, May 1989

I.S.B.N. 84-378-1354-9

Dep. Legal B. 22850-1989

Map of North Africa, engraved in the 16th century.

INTRODUCTION

In eastern Maghreb a coastline of 1,300 km is the Mediterranean boundary of Tunisia, a territory of 164,000 km^2. The word Maghreb means a western Arab country as opposed to Mashriq, an eastern Arab country. It comprises Morocco, Algeria, Tunisia and Libya; a veritable island enclosed by the Mediterranean, the Atlantic Ocean, the Sahara and the Libyan desert.

The glorious past of Tunisia today contrasts with its relatively small size. It can be regarded as African, Mediterranean, Maghreb, Arab-Moslem and Berber. This is an extremely rare characteristic because very few countries can present such an interesting mosaic of cultures. ''The personality of Tunisia derives in large part from its geographical position''. It is in fact a crossroads of different civilisations which lies open both before the oriental and occidental basins of the Mediterranean, at the threshold of Europe, within easy reach of the islands scattered in the east and west of the Mediterranean. The mainland is a place of human intercourse: commercial and cultural currents which arrive from the east, the south through the Sahara, or from the western part of North Africa meet there and intermingle.

The landscape has created favourable conditions for settlement as plains and low hills of a height of less than 200 metres cover almost half of the territory of Tunisia. The Dorsal, the highest range of mountains traverses the country diagonally from the south-west to the north-east. Its summit, Jebel Chambi reaches a height of 1,544 metres. The Tellian Atlas outcrop is in the land of Khroumiry, Nefzas and the Mogods. The country can be divided into three large regions: the land of the plains which in the past was responsible for making Tunisia the granary of Rome which extends to the Dorsal, and the Sahel (olive tree region). Below the Dorsal extends the Steppe zone which towards the south in turn gives way to the Sahara region.

Bordered by the sea in the north and east, the Sahara in the south and the continent in the west, Tunisia enjoys a mild climate throughout the year.

Nevertheless, the north is cold and rainy in the winter, and the weather is variable during the cold season. It is very mild throughout the country during the autumn and spring. In the summer, despite the fresh sea breezes, temperatures may rise to 40° C, while the hot desert wind, the sirocco, blows for a short period.

Rainfall is variable. North of the Dorsal, there is more than 400 mm of rain a year. South of the Dorsal, it is much drier, progressing gradually from a steppe climate to a desert climate in the south, moderated on the coast by the influence of the sea.

The climatic variation is also reflected in the variations in the flora, holm oak and cork oak in the north, the grain growing region in the Tell, large expanses of olive groves in the Sahel, vast fields of alfa grass in the centre west, giving place gradually to orchards, *chotts* (salt lakes) and oases in the south.

The Tunisian population is going through an important demographic development. The birth rate has been increasing since independence, but a birth control programme is gradually being introduced. The population now stands at approximately 7,750,000. Half of the population consists of young people under the age of twenty. One third of the population is urban, which accounts for the development of the capital and the coastal towns, notably Sfax and Sousse. The government has provided free compulsory education since independence, thus furnishing the country with educated personnel in all sectors (administrative, industrial and others).

The people of Tunisia are attached to the Mediterranean, the Sahara, the Orient and the Occident. Tunisia, the crossroads of civilisations has imbued its people with Arab-Moslem traditions, harmoniously enriched with a western culture. Just like the country in which they live, the people of Tunisia can be easily approached whatever the origin of the visitor.

Because of the Arab-Islamic culture and the fact that it is a Moslem country, Tunisia celebrates all Moslem feasts with fervour. All the religious feasts, the Ramadan (month of fasting), Aïd Es Seghir which follows it, Aïd El Kebir (sheep sacrifice), the Mouled (the Prophet's birthday) are many important occasions which unite the Tunisians who are a large Moslem community. Since the political change of 7 November 1987, Tunisia has once again become rooted in its traditions and personality.

THE PREHISTORIC PERIOD

Two million years ago, in the very early days of mankind human beings undoubtedly left the indelible traces of their presence on Tunisian soil. Sharpened pebbles and flint have been found in the fossiferous deposits at Kebili in the south which go back to that period. This can be regarded as the prelude to the entry of all prehistoric civilizations on Tunisian land. However, a dark period persists in the prehistoric period of this country. Between 2 million and 500,000 years ago the absence of deposits does not allow us to follow man's evolution on this land. In the palaeolithic period, Tunisia enters "the hand-axe civilization" in which the pebbles and stone fragments present cuttings on both sides. The Acheulean civilization represented in Tunisia by the Sidi Zin site, close to Le Kef in the Tunisian north-west, goes back to that period. The small axe, a typical tool of that period, is characteristic of the industry of this civilization.

The later palaeolithic period 100,000 years ago succeeds the middle palaeolithic. Two civilizations with close ties, the Mousterian and Aterian succeed the Acheulean. On the Guettar site, in the surroundings of Gafsa, a monument composed of stone balls, flint and bones, piled up in the water at a spring, attests to the birth of religious feeling in the Neanderthal man, in the 40th millenium, when man's preoccupations had by that time passed the subsistence stage. This monument can be seen in the Bardo Museum. The Iberomaurusian and Capsian civilizations will develop in the epipalaeolithic period which succeeds the palaeolithic with the Homo Sapiens, between 15,000 and 5,000 B.C. The Iberomaurusian which has nothing Iberian in it, is represented by the Mechta El Arbi man (in Algeria) discovered 55 km south-east of Gafsa in Bir Oum Ali. The deposit dates back 14,370 years. Remains of the Capsian period which succeeds it were discovered at El Makta 15 km north of Gafsa. Its "escargotieres" or *ramadiyat* (from *ramad:* ash) are characteristic; the ashes mixed with earth or sand, stones and snails shells indicate the Capsian's dwelling. This civilization which had a stone and flint industry presents its women, probably endowed with fineries, in pierced ostrich egg shells, teeth and shells. Art was also born then; a sculpted figurine in soft limestone represents a feminine head. The forehead and sides of the face are framed by the hair.

The Capsian civilization, by the ancient name of *Capsa,* is divided into two periods: the upper Capsian and the typical Capsian which rarely overlap. The Capsian civilization begins thanks to the protomediterraneans whose physical characteristics resemble very closely those of the Berber populations, in the 8th millenium. This period ends in the 5th millenium. Finally the Neolithic period comes to close this great adventure of prehistoric man before the advent of the historical period and the appearance of writing. This period extended for about five thousand years. The Tunisian Neolithic period has several facets and is responsible for many technical innovations: the cutting of flint into arrowheads, stone polishing and pottery modelling. The men of this civilization, who were of the protomediterranean type, buried their dead according to various customs and applied red ochre (the symbol of vitality) to the skull.

Tunisia moored to the African continent, was the melting pot of a vast number of prehistoric civilizations to which it turns its back to look towards the north, and the Mediterranean. On arriving, the Phoenicians discovered a country where the men buried their dead in dolmenic tombs or in graves dug in the mountain sides, a human background enriched by the several thousand year old contribution of the Libyco-Berbers.

View of the Punic Tophet in Carthage.

THE PUNIC PERIOD

The successive Assyrian invasions of Phoenicia (the present Lebanon) and the Greek peril which posed a threat to their flourishing trade by turning increasingly towards the western Mediterranean, obliged the Phoenicians to establish a colony on the African coast which would be in a position to defend the interests of the whole empire. This occurred at the end of the 9th century B.C. Although the city of Utica was built, according to historical proof in 1101 B.C., it is the foundation of Carthage by the famous Elyssa in 814 B.C., that will allow the Maghrebs, generally speaking, and Tunisia in particular to make their official entry into ''written history''. Carthage will remain one of the main actors on the western Mediterranean stage.

Carthage created a civilization in which the eastern Phoenician element well knew how to harmonize with the native Berber element and eventually stand at the head of an Empire, the territorial boundaries of which included a large part of present Tunisia, some parts of the North African coast, western Sicily, Sardinia, Malta, the Balearic Islands and a part of the Iberian Peninsula.

With the foundation of Carthage, Tunisia was, henceforth, destined to constitute a political, economic and cultural centre for more than ten centuries. The country, however, experienced an upheaval as much at the social and political level as at the economic and religious level.

''The Carthaginians were considered to be well governed, their constitution was in many respects superior to the others''. This was the opinion of the Greek philosopher Aristotle. It is the only non-Greek constitution to be included by this philosopher in the models proposed in his book dedicated to politics. The treatise ''Magon's Agronomy'' was translated into Latin by order of the Roman Senate after the destruction of Carthage in 146 B.C. In this book, Magon proposed a scientific study of agriculture and breeding without neglecting to give his advice on the best way of running a farm.

The Greeks have passed on to us the account of a voyage undertaken by a Carthaginian called Hannon who in the middle of the 5th century B.C. began his voyage with 60 ships, each with 50 rowers, carrying 30,000 people. The voyage was planned to take him as far as Mount Cameroon so that in this way the African coast would be explored by the Carthaginians.

These three examples which come from the Greeks and Romans, who were implacable enemies of the Carthaginians, constitute excellent evidence of the influence exerted by Carthage during that period. The political organization of Carthage, its economic supremacy with its two components agriculture and trade and its bold sailors who buccaneered the Mediterranean and beyond, could only make of Carthage an obstacle to any foreign expansion in the western Mediterranean.

In 535 B.C., the Carthaginians, who were the allies of the Etruscans, defeated the Greeks off Alalia, thus preventing them from settling in Corsica.

In 480 B.C., Amilcar was defeated by the Greeks in Himera in Sicily.

In 398 B.C., Denys of Syracusa declared war on Carthage.

In 310 B.C., Agathocles, tyrant of Syracuse, landed in the Cap Bon but was not defeated. Three years later the Carthaginians defeated the Greeks.

Once the Greek chapter was closed, Rome, that had several alliance treaties with Carthage until then, challenged the North African metropolis on three occasions until it brought about its destruction.

The first Romano-Punic war lasted for 23 years (264-241 B.C.). The seventeen years of the duration of the second war (218-202 B.C.) were the most painful to Rome, the very existence of which was threatened. It was during that war that the famous Carthaginian general Hannibal ''equalled but never surpassed'' stayed in the Italian peninsula for fifteen years after having crossed the Alps with his famous elephants. In 217 and 216 B.C., in the Trasimene Lake and Cannes battles, the Roman troops were almost annihilated and the manoeuvres of general

Hannibal are now inscribed in the history of that war. Scipio's landing in Carthage was what forced the Carthaginians to recall Hannibal to North Africa where he fought the last battle which he lost in 202 B.C., in Zama.

The third and ultimate war, the shortest and most tragic (149-146 B.C.), which saw the defection of a large part of the African cities which allied with Rome, ended with the destruction of Carthage; its ploughed land became accursed; no city could spring up and flourish there, according to the Romans. After having given up their weapons (artillery, elephants) and believing in the conclusion of an honourable treaty with the Romans who had landed in Utica in 149 B.C., the Carthaginians were summoned to abandon the city and settle in the hinterland. Without weapons, disarmed by treachery, but with their honour intact, the Carthaginian Senate declared war. The city was to fight from house to house for three years facing the assaults of the soldiers of another Scipio before giving up. Even though Carthage had died the Punic civilization survived; for more than three centuries after the destruction of the city, the Punic writing still remained engraved on the steles. Baal Hammon always watched over the legacy of Carthage to the civilization of the whole world.

THE MASSYLE KINGDOM

The political authorities of Carthage did not administer the whole of the Tunisian territory. Since the 3rd century B.C., historical sources have quoted the existence of the Massyle Kingdom the delimitation of which remains difficult to undertake. Its territory included part of west Tunisia and east Algeria. In the 2nd century B.C., at the time of the Romano-Carthaginian conflict, taking advantage of the weakening of the Carthaginians, Massinissa reigned in a territory which included Tunisia, the Dorsal, a large part of the valley of Medjerda which is not very big, and the Tunisian coast south of Sfax from Thaenae as far as Tripolitania. During that period, Dougga, Maktar and Bulla Regia, for example, were part of that kingdom. However, this kingdom slowly disintegrated after Jugurtha was defeated, in 105 B.C., by the Romans and became a second Roman Province, apart from the ancient Carthaginian territory, in 46 B.C.

THE ROMAN PERIOD

VENARI — LAVARI — LUDERE — RIDERE — OCC EST VIVERE. ''Hunting, baths, games, pleasure, that is what is called to live''. The truth of this Latin inscription discovered in the forum of Timgad in Algeria seems to have been confirmed by the reality and quality of life lived during that period as attest the monuments and mosaics found in this country.

Once Carthage was destroyed, Rome appropriated its territory which only included, at the time, about one fifth of the area of present day Tunisia including the low valley of the Medjerda, the valley of Oued Miliane and the Sahel as far as Sfax. This territory which is separated from the Numidian zone by a ditch, the fossa (Fossia Regia), had Utica as its capital.

The war fought by Jugurtha against Rome which lasted from 110 to 105 B.C. in the Numidian part of the Tunisian territory, was one of the rare periods of trouble in Africa until the civil war which brought into conflict Julius Caesar and Pompey and his allies. The struggle for power in Rome moved to Africa where a decisive battle took place, which put an end to this conflict in 46 B.C., near Thapsus, nowadays El Bekalta, south of Monastir. Caesar's victory ended the existence of the neighbouring Numidian Kingdom the sovereign of which, Juba, had allied with his adversaries. The Numidian territory then became a new African Roman province (Africa Nova) next to the ancient territory of Carthage, Africa Vetus, till 36 B.C., the date of their reunification into one province: Africa Proconsularis. It is thanks to Caesar that the city of Carthage was born again from its ashes. In 44 B.C., he decided to create a Roman colony on the site of the Punic capital. This task was finished only in 29 B.C., by Octavius, the future emperor Augustus.

It is not necessary to be a historian or an archaeologist to appraise the expansion of Tunisia during the Roman period. The whole country constitutes a living museum where the remains from the north to the south attest to the importance of the position held by Tunisia within the Roman Empire.

Tunisia was above all considered to be the granary of Rome. The holds of the ships that left for Ostia were filled with wheat and oil to the point of breaking, to feed the Roman plebeians. But, Tunisia was also the country of cities of which there were over 200. These cities mostly of Punico-Numidian origin constituted one of the factors of romanisation. Following the example of Rome, they built capitols, the political and religious symbol of Rome, where the enthroned statues of Jupiter associated with Juno and Minerva were placed. The *fora* (singular: *forum*),

Mosaic depicting Dionysos children fighting against the pirates, 3rd century A.D.

public squares forbidden to chariots and associated with the capitols, multiplied and became meeting places and centres for the settlement of public and private affairs. Summer and winter baths, circuses, theatres, and amphitheatres made of every city a small copy of Rome. The native bourgeoisie constituted the mainspring of this romanisation and their efforts to become integrated into the wheels of this process, were always successful. Thus, the African cities became first *municipia* and the status of their inhabitants was an intermediate stage between that of being a Roman citizen and that of being a foreigner. Access to the status of a colony would allow them to become Roman citizens. In the 2nd century A.D., 15 per cent of the senators and knights of the whole Roman empire which had reached its climax, were Africans. In 238 A.D., the inhabitants of Thysdrus, the Thysdritans, declared emperor Maximus deposed and proclaimed Gordian the new emperor; from this gesture one can appraise the importance assumed by Africa and above all Tunisia within the Empire.

Tunisia acquired an impressive network of roads, aqueducts, cisterns, farms and olive presses which attest that the occupation of the country was as organised as that of the cities. Contrary to what one may believe, at the time when crisis was rife in some regions of the Roman Empire, Africa was at the peak of its prosperity with the Severi (193-235 A.D.). In the 4th century, the municipal inscriptions multiplied and even though no new cities were created, urban and municipal life persisted.

Tunisia was not only Roman but also Christian. At the time when Gaul offered its first martyrs, the African church could already count tens of bishops. African Christianity, evidence of which is scattered all over Tunisia, is an example of the transfer of culture from the south to the north, from Africa to Europe. St Augustine bears witness to that.

However, in spite of all its splendour, the romanisation which always relied on the local elite, does not seem to have impregnated all the classes of the population, who in the least upheaval turned away from it. The Empire was already in a crisis when Genseric at the head of the Vandal hordes began the conquest of North Africa.

THE VANDAL AND BYZANTINE PERIOD

The Vandal period which Tunisia experienced for one century did not bring a big transformation to the structure of ancient Tunisia.

Genseric who swept through North Africa from the Iberian peninsula in 429 A.D. and seized Carthage in 439 A.D., maintained the Roman administration. The privileges of the defeated were transferred to the winners. Agriculture and trade did not decline and marble was imported from the east to embellish the Christian basilicas and decorate the public buildings and the houses. However, at the religious level, the Vandals, who were Christians professing Arianism, saw a resistance on the part of the traditional Catholics being set up against them. This moral and social crisis was one of the reasons for the collapse of the Vandal power. In 530 A.D., king Hilderic an ally of the Byzantine Emperor Justinian II, was evicted from power by Gelimer. The Byzantines decided to react and their design was to eliminate the Vandals completely.

Between 533-534 A.D. the Byzantines reconquered North Africa but although the Roman Empire installed itself again, it was not to last for long.

What is there to say about the Byzantine period? The most eloquent evidence on that period of the history of Tunisia is of an archaeological character. This evidence consists of fortresses mostly built with reused materials extracted from other buildings. These fortifications were not only built at the crossroads and ways of access, but also in the interior of the country. This denotes a considerable effort in proportion to the danger the country had to face. The Berbers, in effect, lifted up the torch of insurrection. Byzantine policy continued the Roman and Vandal policies of the imposition of taxes which bred social discontent and unrest. The corruption of the executives which was added to this created the conditions for the fall of the Byzantines. But the destiny of Tunisia and North Africa was already determined; the banner of Islam thousands of kilometres away heralded a new era.

THE ISLAMIC FATH (THE BIRTH OF ISLAM)

The battle of *Sufetula* (Sbeitla) in which the patrician Gregory, who was a symbol of the Byzantine power, died in front of Abdallah Ibn Saad in 647 A.D., was only the prelude to the conquest of Ifriqiya.
The arrival of Okba Ibn Nafa in 670 A.D. and the foundation of Kairouan, the first capital of Islam on African soil, did not put an end to the resistance of

The courtyard of the Great Mosque of Kairouan.

the Berbers, who were compelled in the circumstances to become the allies of the Byzantines. Kosseila, a Berber chief, succeeded in killing Okba in 683 A.D. on Algerian soil. From 686-702 A.D. four campaigns had to be undertaken to crush Kosseila, seize Carthage and above all defeat El Kahena, the Berber queen who had been resisting the Islamic conquest for a long time.

THE ORIGINS OF THE REIGNING DYNASTIES

In the early period of Islam, Tunisia appertained to the central power situated either in Damascus with the Ommeyades, or Baghdad with the Abbassids. It then became politically autonomous with five dynasties, lasting until the proclamation of the republic.
The Aghlabid dynasty founded by Ibrahim Ibn Al Aghlab is of Arab origin. The Fatimids came to power thanks to the Berber tribes, but claimed to be descended from Ali and Fatma, the daughter of the Prophet, and thus of Arab origin. The Zirid and the Hafsid dynasties are both of Berber origin, while the Husseinite dynasty is of Turkish origin.

THE AGHLABID PERIOD

Originally Tunisia was an Ommeyad province, later it was ruled by the Abbassids but it was not until the advent of the Aghlabids that the country achieved real stability. Ibrahim Ibn Al Aghlab, who was at first a vassal of the Abassids proclaimed the independence of Tunisia. The Aghlabid dynasty reigned for one century (800-909 A.D.); a golden century indeed for the country during which prestigious monuments were erected in the cities e.g. mosques, monuments for the defence of the cities (ribats), aqueducts, pools etc. Under Ibrahim II a new capital, Raqqada, was built a few kilometres from Kairouan. But Raqqada did not remain a capital for long. Under this dynasty Sicily was again united to North Africa. Palermo was conquered in 831 A.D. and when Taormina was also seized in 902 A.D. the whole island fell to Ibrahim. The Imam Sahnoun, a Malekite theologian, made of Kairouan a temple of knowledge of the same rank as Medine and Al Kufa. But like all ancient dynasties the Aghlabid did not end without bloodshed.

THE FATIMID PERIOD

Al Mahdi, Obeid Allah, was enthroned in 910 A.D., in Raqqada, after Abu Abd Allah, a shiite missionary, had put an end to the reign of the Aghlabid dynasty with the help of the Berber tribe, Kotama.
For the shiites, a Moslem sect, the only legitimate caliphs were the descendants of Ali (the Prophet's cousin and son in law) and Fatma. Thanks to the Fatimids the shiite sect could take its revenge on history; having failed to establish a dynasty in the Orient it would succeed in doing so in the Occident. The capital was transferred from Raqqada to an impregnable peninsula where the city of Mahdia (from the name Al Mahdi) was founded. Such a city would allow this dynasty to take shelter in any internal uprising and also have an opening to the sea. Al Mansour (949-953 A.D.) built a new capital in the Kairouan suburbs: Sabra Al Mansouriya in a country which was now at peace.
However, for the Fatimids the conquest of power in Ifriqiya was only one stage further towards a more glorious destiny, the conquest of the caliphate the way to which passed through Egypt. Under Al Moizz (953-975 A.D.), Egypt became Fatimid. In 973 A.D.

the centre was moved to Cairo leaving the government of Ifriqiya in the hands of a vassal, the chief of the Sanhaja tribe, Bologuin Ibn Ziri.

THE ZIRID PERIOD

The Zirids remained vassals of the Fatimids in a flourishing country until 1048 A.D. when Al Moizz, the Zirid, turned away from the Fatimid power of Cairo and recognised the suzerainty of the Abassids of Baghdad. This episode is a turning point in the history of Tunisia. The Fatimid sovereign punished this betrayal by granting Ifriqiya to the Arab tribes of Beni Hillal, and thereafter to Beni Souleim. It was the beginning of the end for the Zirids and peace and prosperity in Tunisia. These tribes razed to the ground a large part of the country and of course all traces of civilisation. The Zirids managed to preserve only Mahdia from which they were expelled by the Normans in 1148 A.D. The Beni Kourassan governed Tunis.

THE HAFSID PERIOD

Order was established again only in 1159 A.D. during the period of the Almohads who started from Morocco for the conquest of the whole of North Africa. Tunis became the capital of the Almohad governor who had to face a lot of opposition from the Arab tribes.
The appointment of Mohammed Ibn Abi Hafs, a man of considerable calibre, as governor brought peace to the country again.
His son Abou Zakaria (1229-1249 A.D.) proclaimed his independence and thus a new dynasty was born which was one of the longest in the history of Tunisia, as it persisted until 1570 A.D.

By the time this dynasty had reached its climax a large part of Algeria was under its control and the Hafsid sovereign's authority was recognised by all the Moslem suzerains. In the reign of Al Moustansir, Saint Louis landed in Carthage to die there on the 25th of August 1270 A.D., so that the Crusaders' adventure in Tunisia ended as rapidly as it began. During the reign of the Hafsids the country benefitted both in the field of agriculture and of the crafts from the presence of the Andalusians who had fled from Spain which was gradually being converted into a Christian country. Tunis the new capital developed in all sectors after the Almohad interlude.
After the first stream of sovereigns, the Hafsid dynasty fell into anarchy in spite of some bright intervals especially under Abu Faris Al Hafsi (1393-1433 A.D.). The country suffered for a longtime. The new masters of the Mediterranean the Turks and Spaniards installed and deposed sovereigns according to their sympathies or rather their interests.

THE TURKISH PERIOD

At the time when Hafsid Tunisia was slowly disintegrating the Barbarossa brothers from *Myteline,* ancient Lesbos, established piracy in the western Mediterranean as a new political and economic system. Each of the coastal cities became a small state and a basis for their lucrative naval and at the same time religious activities because piracy was also considered to be a holy war directed against the Christians.
Although Arouj, the eldest of the Barbarossa brothers, had won the favour of the Hafsid princes, his younger brother Khair ed Dine who had the protection of the Sublime Porte, was an implacable enemy. He attacked Tunis which was seized on 18

August 1534. This success provoked a reaction on the part of the Christians. Charles the Fifth with an army of 30,000 men and a navy of 400 ships entered Tunis victoriously on 14 July 1535. Thus, Moulay Hassen the Hafsid sovereign regained his unsteady throne. The rivalry between the Turks and the Spanish resulted in Tunis being seized and in 1574 Sinan Pasha annexed Tunisia to the Sublime Porte. A Turkish system of pashas, beys and deys was established without the much desired stability being achieved until the arrival of Murad Bey (1612-1631), a Corsican renegade, who succeeded in obtaining the right to transfer his charge to his descendants. The Muradite dynasty persisted despite all the odds until 1705 when the last of its members, after a fratricidal war allowed Hussein Ben Ali, chief of the janissaries, to establish the Husseinite dynasty which was the last one in the history of Tunisia.

THE HUSSEINITE PERIOD

Hussein Ali, a christian renegade of Greek origin, chief of the janissary militia, established this new dynasty in which the power was transferred from male to male and according to seniority among his descendants.

The Husseinite dynasty was discredited in the eyes of many Tunisians because it had indirectly contributed to the establishment of the protectorate. The different beys, with a few exceptions, became rather uneasy as they had to watch over their personal interests rather than those of the state.

Ahmed Bey (1837-1855) had a progressive policy. He created a school of war to train officers as well as to develop a small military industry (gunpowder factories, foundries, etc.). In August 1858 Tunis had its first municipal council. Under Mohammed Sadok Bey the country was endowed with a constitution

in January 1861 which allowed the institution of a supreme legislative council of 60 members, apart from the Bey.

The country, however, had to follow its destiny. The fact that the state had incurred debts, the unscrupulous bankers, and the corrupt advisers of the Bey, compelled the French, the Italians and the English to seek to protect the interests of their compatriots, the creditors of the Bey, by creating an international commission of finance in 1869 composed of Tunisians and foreigners. This commission acted until 1884 as the ministry of finance which divided the revenue of the regency into two parts; one reserved for the state and the other for the creditors. In spite of the presence of a great reformer, minister Khair ed Dine, the fate of Tunisia had already been decided elsewhere.

It is due to this minister that the first modern school of the country was created. The Sadiki Secondary School (College Sadiki) appeared for the first time on 13 January 1875. It was destined to train the elite who rebelled against the protectorate.

And indeed the fate of Tunisia was decided in Europe. At the Congress of Berlin in 1878 France obtained the backing of the other European powers to conquer Tunisia. The Colonial period began on 24 April 1881 with the entry of a contingent of 35,000 men who occupied Le Kef on 26 April 1881. On the same day a naval division shelled and occupied Tabarka.

THE PROTECTORATE

On 12 May 1881, general Breart presented himself to the French consul Roustan in front of the Bardo Palace. The Bey signed the treaty of Bardo which deprived him of any external sovereignty and a large part of his internal sovereignty. An almost general insurrection followed. La Marsa convention signed on 8 June 1883 allowed France to put Tunisia definitively under its trusteeship. The Bey was retained simply to justify the Protectorate in the eyes of public opinion. The resident minister was the real ruler.

COMBATANT TUNISIA

The new intellectual elite who received a modern education and were dispersed in all directions by the Sadiki School, did not have the opportunity to be employed by the French administration. Since the late 19th century they had, however, queried issues that concerned the majority of the Tunisians, thus contributing to the creation of a ''Tunisian public spirit''. The national conscience, which had never disappeared was born again within the Tunisian society. The first Tunisian nationalists were: Beshir Sfar (1856-1918), the pioneer of the Tunisian national movement, Ali Bach Hamba (1876-1918) and Abdelaziz Thaalbi, founder in 1919 of the Tunisian party which was transformed in 1920 into the Tunisian Constitutional Liberal Party, famous under the name of Destour. The labour movement with the Tunisian Labour General Confederation (CGTT) which had at its head Mohammed Ali Al Hammi, founder of the Tunisian National Trade Union in 1924, shows the other face of Tunisian nationalism. At the congress of Destour in 1933, young Tunisians, mostly of provincial origin, were appointed to the administrative section of the party. After having studied in Paris, they were inspired by the new militant methods from Europe. The two brothers Habib and Mohammed Bourguiba, Bahri Guiga, Tahar Sfar, Mohammed el Matri henceforth represented the radical wing of Destour, the methods of which diverged entirely from those advocated by the partisans of the wait and see policy commended by the party elders. The rupture was confirmed at Ksar Kellal Congress on 12 March 1934 by the creation of a new party, the Neo Destour.

The fight which had gone on occasionally until then, was to intensify with the new political organisation which was now associated with all the active forces of the nation. The martyrs of 9 April 1938 very eloquently bear witness to this.

Despite the fact that during the Protectorate period a lot of development took place and many roads and public works were constructed, the air of reform blowing through Europe and the rest of the world could not leave Tunisia unaffected.

INDEPENDENCE

Tunisia gained its independence on 20 March 1956. On 24 July 1957 Mohammed Lamine Bey brought the Husseinite reign to an end in Tunisia. The republic was proclaimed on the 25th of the same month with Habib Bourguiba as first president. In 1959, the country was provided with a constitution which was later amended in order to allow the president to remain in office for life. On 7 November 1987, and in accordance with Article 57 of the same constitution, the Prime Minister Zine Al Abidine Ben Ali, after the consultation of doctors who certified that Bourguiba would be unable to continue in office due to ill health, was sworn in as second president of the country. On 12 July 1988 the constitution was amended again in order to permanently settle the problems of the presidency; the duration, the re-election of the president and the succession.

Despite the problems faced by all countries that have recently achieved their independence Tunisia, nevertheless, remains a model of development.

Map of Tunis, engraved in the 16th century.

THE MEDINA OF TUNIS

The Medina of Tunis effectively brings the Orient to the gateway of Europe. It was once surrounded by thick walls of which only a few traces remain. However, some of the gates are still well preserved. One may enter the Medina starting from the Bab al Bahr (Gate of France) and continue along the Jamaa Ez Zitouna street, along the east-west axis of the Medina at the heart of the city which leads to the Great Mosque (Jamaa ez Zitouna). It is from here, that the development of the souks, market streets, began. The Great Mosque is surrounded by souks, divided according to the craft guilds. Beyond the commercial inner circle are diverse residential quarters, whose architectural style renders Tunis one of the most beautiful medinas in the Moslem world, a veritable jewel of the Arab-Moslem heritage.

Tunis, Thunes or *Tynes* in antiquity, was a neighbouring city of the Carthaginian metropolis, and was often involved in the diplomatic and military adventures of the Carthaginian empire. From the 11th century on, and following the institution of the principality of the Khorassanids, of which it was the capital,

Tunis became one of the leading cities of Ifriqiya. And while remaining a capital the city flourished especially during the Khorassanid and Hafsid periods. The ruins of neighbouring Carthage served as a quarry, and blocks of finished marble, columns, capitals, lintels, etc., were used to adorn and embellish the religious buildings and imposing palaces of Tunis.

The Great Mosque Ez Zitouna, built in 732 is the oldest moslem place of worship in Tunis.

Access to the portico is via the large steps on the long façade. The building has a library, a large courtyard flanked by a colonnade with ancient capitals, and a vast prayer room, open only to Moslems.

The arches of the latter are supported by an impressive number of ancient columns. The ribbed dome of the mihrab is embellished with stones of two colours and decorated with rich coatings of stucco. From its construction until independence, the Ez Zitouna Mosque was a great centre of Islamic education, and was considered to be among the oldest in the world, and its cultural influence spread throughout the Arab-Moslem world centuries before European universities were founded.

The proximity of the souks to the mosque was determined by the craft. High class crafts such as jewellers were situated close while noisy trades such as saddlers and metal workers were located further away. Some of the more interesting souks are:

Souk el Attarine (perfumers'souks). Display cases are crowded with glass phials, full of natural oils, intoxicating perfumes, baskets full of henna, and other natural cosmetics, the scents of which have enchanted poets throughout the ages.

Souk el Fekka (dried fruits) a colourful souk, with big baskets piled high with dried fruit and delicacies, veritable cornucopias.

Souk el Koumach (materials). The shelves of the shops are full of colourful rolls of silk, veils, foutas and other materials spun in the workshops of Tunis.

Souk el Leffa (wool) is given over to extremely fine rugs and blankets. Woollen products from all the regions of Tunisia (Kairouan, Tozeur, Gafsa, etc.) are available here.

Souk el Berka (goldsmiths), features beautiful showcases gleaming with gold jewellery and gems.

Souk es Sakkajine (saddlers), in the past craftsmen here specialised in fine leather goods. Only a few shops remain.

Souk ech Chaouachiyas (chechias, military caps). This craft was introduced in Tunisia in the 17th century by an Andalusian family and it has been flourishing ever since. Despite the loss of a large part of the local market, exports have allowed the craft to continue.

Souk el Blaghjia (babouches-Turkish slippers) specialises in the making of modern and traditional shoes.

Souk of the Ladies: venue for the sale of second hand goods.

A short distance from the Great Mosque in a north-easterly direction is the square of the Kasbah, or square of the government, which has for long been the centre of administration, situated on the outskirts of the Medina. Several departments of the government, including the prime minister's office and the ministry of foreign affairs are concentrated in the various palaces, situated around the square. The Kasbah was originally a citadel, converted by the Hafsids and divided into three sections: the palaces, the administrative buildings and the barracks.

Further to the south is Dar Hussein, an Arab palace, originally built in the 18th century, and modified several times. It now houses the National Institute of Archaeology and Arts. This sumptuous house has two courtyards framed by colonnades and marble paving. The arches are supported by columns with Corinthian capitals, the ceilings are in painted wood. The inner walls are decorated with rich coatings of stucco, and ceramic tiles. This princely edifice also has an interior garden.

In the southern part of the Medina is Dar Ben Abdallah palace which now houses the museum of folk and popular art.

The remaining and best preserved gates of the Medina are:

Bab el Bahr (Gate of France). This was one of the gates in the ramparts originally surrounding the Medina. The gate was modified several times, and in its current form dates back to 1848.

Bab el Jedid. This gate was built in 1276 in the ramparts of the Medina of Tunis, and is a beautiful example of the architecture of the Hafsid period.

Bab el Khadra. Well preserved, this gate is found in the northern, outer suburbs of Tunis.

The Zawiya of Sidi Qasim Az Zaligi (late 15th century). The name of this mausoleum indicates that it was the work of an Andalusian potter (zalig means glazed wall tiles). Built in the Spanish-North African style, with a sloping roof, covered in green glazed tiles, the interior of the building is richly decorated with worked stucco, ceramic tiles, marble columns and capitals. The mausoleum has been converted into a museum, featuring collections of ceramics, moslem funeral steles and inscriptions in Kufi writing.

The courtyard of the Dar Ben Abdallah museum.

THE DAR BEN ABDALLAH MUSEUM

The palace of Dar Ben Abdallah built in the 18th century, in a style much influenced by the Italian architecture of the time was reconverted in the early 19th century. It now houses the museum of Folk Art and Traditions. The museum has four rooms, each depicting the diverse cultural aspects of Tunisia in the 19th and 20th centuries. One room marks the important stages in the life of a Tunisian child. Two rooms trace the life of women representing a wedding featuring collections of jewels, toiletries, chest and jewel boxes. A woman's daily life, her needle work and clothes are also evoked. The last room is reserved for men, featuring costumes, especially those of the Hanefi and Maleki Imams and other articles such as beads, snuffboxes, etc.

The entrance to the museum.

Customs of Tunisia:
Three views of the
museum.

View of the Great Mosque.
The inner courtyard of the Dar Hussein Palace.
The Zawija of Sidi Qasim Az Zaligi.
Government square: the kasbah.

The gate leading to the mosque of El Ksar and the Dar
Hussein Palace.
Bab El Khadra.
Gate of France (Bab el Bahr).
Bab el Jedid.

Views of the souks of the Medina.

Views of the Medina.

A 16th century engraving of Tunis.

THE NEW CITY

Besides its attractive and charming medina, Tunis also has an agreeable modern section. The main street is Habib Bourguiba Avenue, which runs from the port on the lake of Tunis to Avenue de France, and reaches the Gate of France (Bab el Bahr). The avenue is lined with ficus, and its central footpath teems with people, while florists arrange their flowers from morning to evening on their part of the pavement. On the southern side of the avenue is the municipal theatre, built in 1911, with its imposing banister. The bronze statue of Ibn Khaldoun is situated between Saint Vincent de Paul's cathedral, built in 1882 and the French embassy, formerly the General Residence at the time of the Protectorate, and level with Independence Square. At the far end, at the intersection of Turkey Street and Mohammed Avenue is 7 November Square. The square, formerly known as Africa Square and for a short time 3 August Square, is the site of an imposing four sided clock which strikes up the national anthem. This immense clock has replaced the equestrian statue of Habib Bourguiba.

In the afternoon, thousands of sparrows settle down on the trees of the avenue.

From 7 November Square starts Mohammed V Avenue, fast becoming the financial centre of the city. This avenue links the city with the banks of the lake where a new nucleus of office buildings and banks, some like the Central Bank of Tunisia built in a modern style, is slowly developing.

The construction of a conference centre has made this road one of the most important of the city. Pasteur Square, at the end of Mohammed V Avenue bordering on Belvedere Park is a huge green island in the midst of the concrete and a source of fresh air for the people of Tunis.

Worth visiting is the zoo. Visitors can savour a moorish coffee, amidst the trumpeting of the elephants and the quacking of the ducks. The latter also tend to waddle over to the table and beg for a piece of bread or "kaki".

The more adventurous should make sure to visit the Koubba, a pavilion with open galleries on its three sides. The vaults and arches of the Koubba are decorated with carved plaster, adorned with small colourful stained glass windows. The elegant building combines with the beauty of the landscape to make this spot one of the emblems of Tunis.

Hotel capacity in Tunis has grown spectacularly both in quality and in quantity over the past few years as part of the avowed aim of Tunisia to become a key centre for international conferences and business travellers.

Although it is already the headquarters of the government, the Arab League, and Alecso, Tunis has great prospects of becoming a successful tourist centre. No visit to Tunis is complete without visiting the Bardo Museum which is reputed to possess the largest collection of Roman mosaics in the world.

BARDO MUSEUM

Bardo museum, which celebrated its 100th year in 1988, holds a special place in the cultural life of the country, and attracts more than 500,000 visitors a year.

Situated in a western suburb of Tunis, Bardo was the seat of power of the beys for more than a century. The museum is housed in one of the palaces built by Mohammed Bey between 1855 and 1859. He then abandoned it for another residence. On 7 May 1888 it became a museum and took the name of Musée Alaoui after the sovereign of the time, Ali Bey (1882-1902). With independence in 1956 it became the national museum, and was renamed "Bardo National Museum".

Visitors will be impressed by the beauty of its magnificent ceilings, made of either finely cut and decorated plaster panels, or vividly coloured carved wood.

Bardo museum traces the history of Tunisia, from prehistoric to modern times. But it is especially noteworthy for its mosaics, featuring the largest collection of Roman mosaics in the world, from the most important sites in Tunisia: Carthage, Hadrumetum (Sousse), Dougga, Thysdrus (El Djem), Uthina (Oudna), Acholla (Botria), etc. Separate rooms are reserved for representative mosaics from each of these sites. Mosaics are also exhibited in other rooms by theme, such as hunting, amphitheatre games, etc. Important exhibits include the unique portrait of the Latin poet Virgil. The mosaic comes from Sousse and

Mosaic depicting Ulysses and the sirens, 3rd century A.D.

Bas-relief of eight goddesses, 3rd to 1st century B.C.

A Libyco-Latin funerary stele.

dates back to the second century A.D. It portrays a seated Virgil, holding a papyrus inscribed with verse eight of the Aeneid on his knees.

The Greek epic poet Homer, and the legendary hero of the Odyssey, Ulysses, are among the museum's most famous pieces. Ulysses is portrayed tied to the mast of a ship, seeking to escape from the siren's songs, surrounded by his companions.

Holding their shields, with their ears blocked with wax, the sirens are shown playing their double flute and lyre on a rock. This piece, of the 3rd century A.D. was found in Dougga.

Among the many pieces from Roman Africa is some paving from Carthage, depicting the life of the

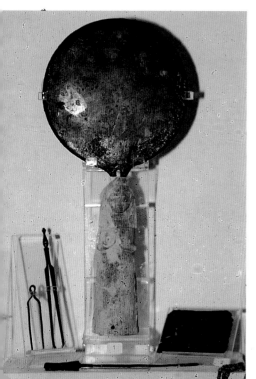

Bronze mirror with ivory base, 7th century B.C.

View of the room with Roman-Carthage exhibits.

Statue of Emperor Hadrian, 2nd to 3rd century A.D.

The baptistry, 6th century A.D.

Statue of Creperia Innula, 2nd century A.D.

Virgil's room.

African aristocracy in the 4th century A.D. The mosaic also depicts in detail the large domain of an African aristocrat, Lord Julius.

Equally imposing, both for their size and beauty, are the Roman sculptures. Among the most beautiful in the museum are those of Apollo, Aeschulapius and Ceres, found in the same temple in Bulla Regia. Considered among the most beautiful in the museum is the statue of emperor Hadrian, portrayed as Mars, and the Hercules of Thuburbo Majus portrayed with a lion skin on his head and tied to his chest, and a club in his left hand.

The museum also features other Roman finds, among the funeral and votive steles, sarcophagi, ceramics, glass, bronze, etc.

Prehistoric finds are grouped in a special section. They include, heads, flints, scrapers, dating back to the different prehistoric civilisations of Tunisia, the acheulean, mousterian, arterian and ibero-mauruzian. This section also includes a unique monument, offering the oldest surviving clue of the religious practices of the Neanderthal man. Essentially a heap of stone balls, cut flint, bones and teeth, it was found in an artesian spring at El Guettar, near Gafsa.

The Libyco-Punic exhibits are grouped in four small interconnecting rooms, portraying the Phoenico-Punic and Numidian history of Tunisia.

In one of the rooms is an enthroned terra-cotta figurine, representing the Phoenician god, Baal Hammon, wearing a feathered tiara. Nearby are various steles dedicated to this deity over the course of nine centuries.

The oldest dates back to the 7th century B.C. and bears the most ancient inscription found on Carthaginian soil. The most recent dates back to the 2nd century A.D. It originates from Maktar, the ancient *Mactaris* and indicates that the destruction of Carthage, three and a half centuries earlier (146 B.C.) did not destroy Punic civilisation. The terra-cotta statues, exhibited in the same room, (a goddess with a head of a lion, Demetra, Kore, Pluto) come from a country

Mosaic portrait of Virgil and the two muses, 2nd century A.D.

One of the richly decorated ceilings of the museum.

sanctuary and attest to the importance of the fertility cult among the people of Africa in antiquity. The two following rooms contain fourteen display cases which exhibit fourteen different themes, but all feature an element found inside Punic tombs. The articles ceramics, bronze, ivory, worship and toilet articles come mostly from Punic tombs and are displayed in their original setting. Every showcase is protected by an amulet, used by the Punics to protect themselves against the evil eye.

The exhibits in the fourth room originate in the main from the Massyle territories (north-western and western Tunisia), and date to after the fall of Carthage. One noteworthy item is an inscription commemorating the erection of the temple dedicated to king Massinissa built ten years after his death by his son and successor Micipsa, and written in Punic and Libyc. Also on display are native deities, different from the Punic and Latin ones.

A large part of the museum is reserved for the Moslem period, spanning the middle ages to the present. This department includes a small palace built in 1831-32 under the reign of Hussein Bey II Ben Mahmoud. The palace has a central patio, and fountain.

A large part of this section was renovated in 1987. Exhibits in the "blue" room include ceramics, ivory, weapons, coins, and fabrics, notably Coptic cloth and the famous "tiraz" fabrics, decorated with inscriptions. These fabrics, which belonged to illustrious personalities, date back to the Abbassid (742-1258) and Fatimid periods (909-1170).

Of note are the yellow-copper astrolabes dating back to the 14th century, 1629 and 1772, featuring the signs of the zodiac and the names of the main stars. The signed sundials date to 1778 and 1852.

A room, reconstructed as a traditional reception room, opens onto the small palace patio. In the right alcove of the room is a beautiful bed. The headrest canopy is painted red and bears a golden decoration on relief, executed in a Venetian style, perhaps by

a local craftsman. Two small rooms on both sides of the fountain contain engravings dating back to the 16th century and depicting the campaign of the Spanish King, Charles V in Tunisia. A Spanish inscription commemorates the seizure of Tunis by Charles V in 1535.

This section also features an impressive collection of weapons such as guns and blunderbusses, string and percussion musical instruments, chests inlaid with mother of pearl and ivory.

The room reserved for the Tunisia of the 19th and early 20th centuries includes articles in embossed silver, among them sprayers, *qabqab* (wooden "clogs" covered in silver and worn by the brides of Tunis), and a stick in embossed decoration (used by the bridegroom during the first week of conjugal life).

Patio of the small palace of the museum.

Also on display are costumes, traditional jewels from different parts of the country (Sahel, Cap Bon, Djerba, Tataouine) showing the diversity and wealth of Tunisian heritage. On the ground floor, a large patio and the passage leading to it, are entirely covered with ceramic panels. The tiles include Moroccan tiles, reminiscent of the Roman mosaics, and tiles from Spain, the Middle East and Asia Minor. The Tunisian tiles come from the specialised workshops of Qallaline in the course of the 19th century. These bear floral and some times geometric designs, featuring mosques, animals, lions and birds.

A special room is given over to the submarine excavations of Mahdia, featuring the remains of the cargo of a ship wrecked off Mahdia in 81 B.C., including bronze and marble. These exhibits may perhaps originate from the sacking of Athens by Sylla, some time before it was wrecked. The most representative bronze articles include statues of Eros Androgyne, Hermes Orator, Hermes of Dionysos and candelabras. The sculptures, Pan's head, a playing child, and capitals with initials also date from the 3rd-2nd centuries B.C.

The room of treasures, inaugurated on the 100th anniversary of the museum, glimmers with gold finds spanning 12 centuries. This room is unique in North Africa, and contains jewels representing some of the deities of the Phoenico-Punic pantheon. Two rings represent Baal Hammon and Melqart, the god of Tyre. The scarab seals, in gold settings, depict the Egyptian deities, Isis and Bes. The collection includes a large collection of earrings and necklaces, and a series of small golden cases topped by the lion head of the Egyptian goddess Sekhmet or the head of a she cat, head of the goddess Bastet.

Also exhibited are magic texts, engraved on thin rolls. In order to protect themselves against various perils the Punics would appeal to the magic of the text and the magic of gold. Jewels dating back to the 5th century A.D. testify to the prosperity of the country during the period of the Vandals.

Habib Bourguiba Avenue.

Bab Saadoun.

The Municipal theatre.

St. Vincent de Paul's Cathedral and the statue of Ibn Khaldoun.

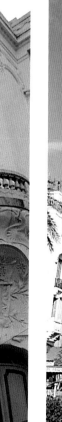

View of Belvedere park.

Pasteur square.   *Africa square.*

View of 7 November square and Mohamed V Avenue.

View of Lake Tunis.

THE NORTHERN SUBURBS OF TUNIS

The northern suburbs of Tunis, with their historical sites, beautiful landscape and traditional character, are an attraction to foreign and local visitors alike. The coastal string of suburbs can be visited by car or the blue train, TGM (the initials of Tunis, Goulette and La Marsa) as the locals tend to call it. The latter links up La Goulette, Carthage, Sidi Bou Said and La Marsa with Tunis.

Starting from 7 November Square the road from Tunis goes through the Lake of Tunis and continues to La Goulette.

La Goulette a very popular and busy resort is also the first harbour of Tunisia. The entrance of the city is dominated by a Spanish-Turkish fortress, used as a jail in the Husseinite period. The main avenue, F. Roosevelt, is lined with restaurants offering sea food delicacies on terraces which are cool even in the middle of the scorching summer season. La Goulette flourished especially in the 1960's and 1970's, when the whole suburb bustled with life and the tunes of such great Tunisian singers as Ali Riahi, Raoul Journou and others.

From La Goulette the road leads to Carthage which jealously guards more than 12 centuries of greatness, and archaeologists have been hard at work decoding them since the late 19th century. A major international archaeological dig was launched in 1974 under the auspices of UNESCO.

From Carthage the road continues to Sidi Bou Said. A gem of Arab-Moslem town planning, it is the pearl of the northern suburbs. A beautiful village it is set high up on the flanks of Jebel el Manar, surrounded by cypress and overlooking a beautiful harbour for sailing boats. A short distance to the north is La Marsa.

La Marsa, now one of the busiest suburbs of Tunis, was in the past a home of the beys. The resort has a beautiful beach, extending as far as Sidi Abdel Aziz. The coastal road with its imposing villas and palmtrees is one of the most charming neighbourhoods of the suburb.

CARTHAGE

Carthage or Quart Hadasht, (the New City), the prestigious city of Elyssa Dido was founded in 814 B.C. by the Phoenicians and flourished for more than six centuries. The home of Hannon the navigator, Magon the master of agriculture, Hannibal the strategist and of beautiful Sophonisbe martyr of the war against Rome, seems to be predestined for glory. Carthage was a Punic capital until it was destroyed by Rome in 146 B.C., which saw it as the biggest threat against its expansion. It was reborn under emperor Augustus, to become *Karthago*, the capital of Roman Africa. It is now the site of the presidential palace of Tunisia.

Once a great Punic capital, and a rival to Rome, Carthage also became the birthplace of Romano-African civilisation. The Tophet, situated in Salammbo on the western edge of the harbour, is the most important Punic sanctuary in the whole of North Africa, and of the whole Phoenico-Punic world. The sanctuary is dedicated to the two main deities of the Carthagi-

The Punic dwellings (Byrsa hill).

nian pantheon, the god Baal Hammon, and the goddess Tanit. It dates back to the second half or mid 8th century B.C., and was frequented by the faithful as a place of pilgrimage from the beginning, through to the fall of Punic Carthage. The sanctuary is made up of an open courtyard with a furnace reserved for sacrifices. Around it are votive steles, driven into the ground, and at the base of which were buried the ceramic urns with the sacrificial ashes. More than 6,000 votive steles have been found at this site. It is believed that the sacrifice of children was not common, and was only practised at the very early stages, and involved children who were either stillborn or died very young. Later on animals were sacrificed at the sanctuary.

Nearby are the two Punic harbours linked by a channel, the first a circular harbour used for military purposes, the second quadrangular and used for com-

The Roman villa.

merce. Two models in the museum illustrate the density of sea traffic and the importance of the harbour to the Punic capital.

Carthage Hannibal was excavated by a German archaeological mission, and contains the only remaining part of the Punic wall, dating back to the 5th century B.C., as well as ruins of Punic paving and architectural fragments.

Further on, within the same area, are the remains of the baths of Antonine, third in rank after those at Caracalla and Diocletian in Rome. Built in the 2nd century A.D. the baths were severely damaged by the Vandals, and only the underground floor is still preserved. The upperfloor, including the diverse thermal annexes were almost entirely demolished. On the way to the museum is the aviary and the theatre. Large in size, it is built on a hill, and is used for performances and a large international festival.

Also worth visiting is the Byrsa quarter. Archaeologists have excavated a large number of Punic dwellings on the southern slope of Byrsa hill, built some 50 years before the fall of Carthage.

The remains cover several blocks of houses, shops and streets, with perpendicular intersections. But the severe drain on the economy of Carthage caused by the wars against Rome is reflected in the simple cesspools which replaced the axial sewer. The houses are usually built with a central courtyard, reached by a gallery. The rooms are built round the yard, which usually contains a cistern.

The national museum of Carthage stands close to the Punic quarter and includes Punic exhibits. Of special note on the ground floor is the beautiful marble anthropoid sarcophagus with sculpted covers, one of them a male representing a recumbent statue on a tomb, and the other a female figure wearing a costume with folded back wings.

The first floor exhibits real treasures of Punic civilisation, notably Phoenician, Punic and imported ceramics, masks, statuettes and a collection of amulets and ivory articles.

SIDI BOU SAID

The village was placed under the protection of a holy man, Abu Said el Beji in 1207. It is a village of whitewashed houses, and blue windows and doors reflecting the blue sky and sea. Crooked cobbled streets wind up the steep slopes while the square bustles with cafes. In the late summer a big religious ceremony takes place every year at the mausoleum of Abu Said el Beji. Known as the *Kharja* or the exit, hundreds of pilgrims and the brotherhoods of Tunis liven up the village with liturgical songs and prayers until dawn.

Views of Sidi Bou Said.

The fortress in La
Goulette.
Two views of
Gammarth.
The entrance to the
Presidential Palace in
Carthage.
View of La Marsa.

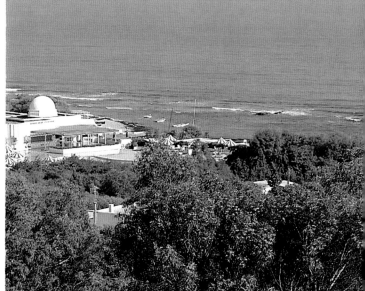

A detail of a mosaic from Utica.

THE NORTH-EASTERN REGION

North-eastern Tunisia boasts some of the most scenic beaches in the country and several places of interest. The P8 from Tunis, via the suburbs of Le Bardo or l'Ariana, leads to Bizerte. At the level of the village of Zhana, a narrow road on the right leads to the site of Utica, the Punic town which became the first Roman capital in Africa.

From Utica 12 km along the P8, the C29 leads to Ghar El Melh. Once a great harbour, Ghar El Melh has been silted up, thus depriving it of a great future. Ghar El Melh (salt cave), previously known as *Porto Farina,* was known as the port of *Rusucmona* in the Punic period. Its strategic location in the bay of Utica led to the erection of fortifications and palaces in the 18th and 19th centuries. But the silting up of its port prevented it from developing into a stronghold of the Tunisian navy.

The harbour enjoyed a distinguished history. It was here that Charles V anchored his navy, in 1541 before attacking Tunis. Ousta Mrad was the first to make Ghar El Melh a real stronghold, turning it into a den for pirates in the 17th century.

The remains of the three forts testify to the importance of the site. The harbour is now only accessible to small fishing boats, and is surrounded by arches on the three sides unique in Tunisia. Not far from Ghar El Melh is Raf Raf.

Raf Raf owes its fame to the muscat grapes cultivated in vineyards extending parallel to the seashore. The small island of Pilau, stands guard opposite a sandy beach.

To reach Bizerte either drive back to the P8, or take the C69E1 which crosses Ras Jebel and links on the P8 to Bizerte.

Bizerte boasts some of the best beaches in the country, among them Rimel beach, with its pine wood, and Corniche beach. But Bizerte has especially made its mark as a harbour, and is the only port in the country where fishing boats are able to penetrate and dock as far as the houses, which seem to protect the sea which laps at their base.

From Bizerte one may continue to Tabarka.

UTICA

Utica, both in the past as in the present, has lived under the shadow of Carthage.

The city was founded by the Phoenicians, in 1101 BC, while on their way to Spain, and served as one of their many harbours which linked the southern coast of the Mediterranean basin. Utica remained independent from Carthage until the 5th century B.C., when it passed under its political influence, while retaining a considerable amount of autonomy. It was considered an ally rather than a subject of Carthage in all the treaties signed by the latter. However, the city was not to prove a very reliable ally. In 149 B.C. it sided with Rome, and in return became the capital of the Roman empire in Africa in the years between the destruction of Punic Carthage and the birth of Roman Carthage. A colony under emperor Hadrian (117-138 A.D.), the city of Utica continued to flourish under the Vandals. Its disappearance coincided with the Islamic conquest.

So far, the only remains of the Phoenician Punic period are the tombs, built of blocks of sandstone or carved in the shape of vats and covered with slabs. No public monuments of the Roman period survive in Utica. But the site contains some distinct houses, unlike those anywhere in Africa. The houses are separated from the streets by a small, narrow yard, which borders the blocks of houses on the four sides, thus protecting the owners from the noisy road.

One of the most remarkable houses of Utica, is the House of the Cascade, a large residence with mosaics featuring fish and fishing scenes. Its paving is a mixture of Chemtou yellow marble, originating from north-west Tunisia, and the green cipolino imported from the Greek island of Eubea. The antiquarium of Utica features objects marking the different stages of life in the city, from the Phoenician Punic period to the end of the Roman period. Of special interest are the collection of Corinthian ceramics and Punic jewels, and especially the ring featuring the god Baal Hammon. Also on display are ceramics, sculptures and mosaics from the Roman period.

View of the remains of Utica.

BIZERTE

Very little remains of the ancient *Hippo Diarrhytus* of Punic and Roman times. Conquered in 661 by the Muslims, the destiny of the city, renamed Bizerte, has remained tied to the sea. Its strategic position in the heart of the Mediterranean made Bizerte an important privateering base until the 17th century. With the beginning of the Protectorate, France installed a naval base, which it retained even after independence. The base was closed in 1963.

Worth visiting are the ramparts and the Kasbah, an old fortress dating back to 17th century, and which, unlike other cities protects only houses. Built at the top of a hill close to the Andalusian neighbourhood is the Fort of Spain, dating back to the Turkish period (Eulj Ali: 1570-73). Now converted into an open air theatre, venue for the Mediterranean song festival, the Fort offers a spellbinding view of the city and of its surroundings, especially the lake.

Ghar El Melh.

Views of Bizerte.

Typical scene of
North-eastern
Tunisia.

Raf-Raf: the Pilau
island.

Typical scenes of
North-eastern
Tunisia.

View of the forest near Aïn Draham.

THE NORTH-WESTERN REGION

The north-western region of Tunisia, with its green and varied landscape, presents a picture few would automatically associate with Tunisia.

From Tunis take the P5 road to Medjez el Bab, and on to Beja.

Beja, a prosperous agricultural city, is set in the middle of fertile plains, in which cereals are grown. The old city, dominated by the Kasbah, is especially noteworthy for its numerous mosques and its souks, where venders sell excellent farm cheese and Beja sweet cakes, *(Mkharak),* packed in pots and sealed with plaster.

From Beja take the P6 to Bousalem and on to Jendouba. Continue towards the Algerian border to Chemtou.

Built on a hill, Chemtou, the Numidian city of *Simithus* flourished under the Romans because of its yellow marble quarry. The site is of archaeological interest, but driving conditions are difficult, and a visit should only be attempted by the more adventurous. Once back in Jendouba, a left turn on to the P17 road leads to Bulla Regia, with its unique underground villas. The P17 road continues to Aïn Draham.

Aïn Draham is built at an altitude of 800 m, and is surrounded by pine and cork oak forests and spiky rocks. The red tile roofed houses of this mountain village are built in a colonial style.

The village is especially popular with visitors during the cool autumn months, and in the winter when the village is one of the only spots in Tunisia where snow falls. The village is also used as a starting point for wildboar hunting.

There are several alternative tracks allowing visitors to discover the secrets of the Khroumiry mountains and visit the Beni M'tir dam, a mountain lake surrounded by green forests.

Visitors to Aïn Draham also have the opportunity to admire the local collection of carved wood and Khroumir rugs.

From Aïn Draham the road continues to Tabarka.

Ruins of the Roman bridge.

CHEMTOU

Built on a high hill, the Numidian city of *Simithus* flourished under the Romans because of its yellow marble quarry. Boosted by the marble of Numidia *(Marmor Numidian)* the city was given the rank of a colony in 27 B.C.

Simithus possesses some distinctive monuments. Among them are:

The sanctuary: This beautiful Numidian temple stands atop a hill. Built in the 2nd century B.C., by King Micipsa, the temple survived to become a sanctuary dedicated to Saturn in the Roman period, then a Christian church, and finally a *marabout* which is still visited today. Fragments of the sculpture decorating the façade are exhibited at the excavations house. The west and north slopes of this holy place perched up high, feature rupestral votive scenes, on steles dedicated to Saturn, that are almost unique in Tunisia.

The quarries: situated at the bottom of God's hill, the marble quarry reveals the quarrying techniques and the size of the block and columns that were extracted from the rock. Each block extracted was inscribed with the name of the reigning emperor, the Roman consul in charge, the zone of the quarry, the administrator responsible and the yearly production. Quarrying of Chemtou marble began in the 1st century B.C. and continued until the Byzantine period.

The work camp: this is the largest complex of workmen's houses, baths, stores, warehouses and workshops excavated to date, and reflect the importance of the imperial quarries. In the workshops the yellow marble was carved into bowls, goblets in relief and statues.

The mill: One of the biggest Roman bridges ever built in Tunisia it is situated west of the Medjerda. On the left bank of the Medjerda are the remains of a grain-mill, operated by watermills unique in the ancient world.

The ruins of the theatre.

View of the theatre.

View of the Baths of Iulia Memmia.

BULLA REGIA

Situated in the fertile "large plains" Bulla Regia was under the sovereignty of Carthage from the 3rd century B.C. It then passed under the control of the Numidian kings. In the Roman period, Bulla Regia was at first a free city, it became a *municipium* in the 1st century B.C., and a colony in the first half of the 2nd century A.D. The social elite of Bulla Regia was well received in the Roman senate.

Bulla Regia differs from other Roman sites of Tunisia because of its underground villas. This ingenious local feature was made necessary by the special weather conditions of the region. The underground floor, reached by well lit stairs, offered an escape from the scorching summer heat, and cold winters.

A good example of architecture and fine mosaics typical to Bulla Regia is the House of the Hunt. The ribbed vault was faithfully reconstructed in the underground room of the New House of the Hunt. Other important buildings in Bulla Regia are the baths and the theatre.

The baths of Iulia Memmia constitute one of the most beautiful public monuments in Bulla Regia. The baths are well preserved, and include several outbuildings. Built in the traditional Roman style, the theatre is also well preserved.

The city is also noted for its collection of sculptures, a large part of which is exhibited at the Bardo museum.

The antiquarium has two rooms, the first reserved for exhibits dating back to the Punic period including ceramics, steles, and coins. The second has a reconstructed tomb, and Roman finds, especially sculptures.

House of the Hunt.

Amphitrite's House.

House of the Fishing.

Detail of a mosaic at Amphitrite's House.

Overall view of Tabarka.

Views of Tabarka including the Genoese fort. ▷

TABARKA

This city combines the beauty of the sea with the charm of the forested Khroumiry mountains.

Its strategic location, and the wealth of its hinterland and rocky coast with their products of cork, wood, coral, and fish, made the ancient city of Tabarka much sought after. Originally an ancient Punic port, it then fell under the control of the Romans. As its numerous religious buildings indicate, Tabarka was one of the most important of the African dioceses during the Christian period. It was occupied by the Genoese in the 16th and 17th centuries, and the Genoese influence can be seen in the ruins of a large fort. From the late 18th century until independence, Tabarka was under French domination.

In recent years, Tabarka has flourished both industrially and touristically. It is the site of a cork factory, and earthenware factory, coral crafts, and workshops producing pipes.

Touristic development has given further impetus to the local economy.

Worth visiting in Tabarka is the basilica, converted from a Roman cistern. The basilica has three naves and also houses a small museum.

Typical scenes of North-western Tunisia.

THE CENTRAL-WESTERN REGION

Some of the most important Roman sites of Tunisia are found in this region among them Dougga, considered to be one of the most spectacular Roman sites of the country.

Maktar, Zaghouan and smaller sites like Le Krib, the Roman *Mustis,* are worth visiting. The landscape of this region is varied. The towns and villages have an interesting architectural character.

The P3 from Tunis passes through the ruins of the Roman aqueduct and a right turn off the P3 into MC133 leads to Zaghouan.

Apart from its proximity to Tunis, Zaghouan and its surroundings are well worth a visit not least for the beauty of the mountainous landscape on which perch several Berber villages, among them Jradou and Zriba, numerous spas, such as Jebel Oust or Hammam Zriba, and the water temple of the city of Zaghouan, the ancient *Ziqua,* a unique monument and a leading tourist attraction.

The temple is situated outside the modern city. On the way is the *marabout* of Sidi Ali Azouz, easily distinguishable by its cupola covered with green glazed tiles. A small triumphal arch recalls the Roman occupation of the site.

From Zaghouan the C28 road leads to the ruins of Thuburbo Majus which are situated at the entrance of the city of the El Fahs, 54 km from Tunis. Originally a small Berber town, the city flourished in the Punic period and sided with Carthage during its last war against Rome.

Its romanisation was rapid, and it acquired the status of a colony at the end of the second century A.D. The city began to decline during the second half of the third century A.D., reaching its nadir in the fifth century.

From Thuburbo Majus the P4 road leads to the Roman site of Maktar through the small town of Siliana. One may continue to Le Kef or alternatively return to Tunis via the same road. From Thuburbo Majus one may reach Testour, taking the C28 road via Goubellat and then C137 or continuing along the C28 from Guebellat to Medjez El Bab and then taking the P5 road towards Testour. The small town of Testour is situated on the Dougga road, on the site of a small Roman village called Tichilla. The town developed in the 17th century following the expulsion of the Moors from Spain.

From Testour the road leads to Teboursouk and the Roman site of Dougga passing through Ain Tounga where the ruins of a Byzantine fortress can be seen. The Roman site of Dougga is considered to be the most important ancient city in north west Tunisia. From Dougga the P5 passes through Le Krib, the Roman *Mustis.* This Roman city is set in the middle of a fertile plain, one kilometre from Krib village, on the great road linking Carthage and Theveste. The city's entrance and exit are marked by two triumphal arches. The city is also the site of the temples to Apollo, Ceres and Pluto, an olive press, a large Roman house and a basilica and a fortress dating back to Byzantine era.

From Le Krib the road continues on to Le Kef.

Le Kef is an attractive city set high up on the southern flank of Dyr el Kef above 700 metres. Its imposing kasbah dominates the city and offers a spellbinding view of the Tellian terrain, which extends as far as Algeria. The town is also a vantage point from which to explore the archaeological sites of the central-west.

View of the aqueduct.

ZAGHOUAN

The water temple of Zaghouan is an imposing monument, built against a cliff and spread out over an immense plain. The temple was built during the reign of emperor Hadrian, and is semi-circular. It is 30 metres in width and 35 metres in length. A cell erected in the centre was supposed to contain the statue of the protective geni of the spring, and twelve niches fitted in to the wall were intended for the nymph statues.

Below, the spring water was collected in a pool before flowing into an aqueduct. Life springs out of this sterile rock as if by magic.

The aqueduct runs parallel to a large part of the road leading to Tunis. Also the work of emperor Hadrian (120-131), it stretches 123 km, ignoring the vicissitudes of time or terrain. The aqueduct allowed the inhabitants of Carthage to quench their thirst at the spring. It was restored several times, e.g. in the Islamic period in the 10th and 13th centuries.

The water temple, Zaghouan.

The capitol.

The gate of the temple of Caelestis.

THUBURBO MAJUS

The capitol is among the most imposing monuments of Thuburbo Majus. The columns of the capital stand out clearly in the horizon, and dominate the forum. A staircase occupies all the width of the building. The façade originally had six fluted Corinthian columns, but only four, of a height of 8.5 m are currently preserved.

The capitol, resembles that of Rome, and is dedicated to the emperors Marcus Aurelius and Commodus. The forum, the focus of public life was 49 metres on each side and covered a total area of 2,400 square metres.

The dimensions of the forum are significant in relation to the size of the city, which covers 40 hectares. It is thus larger than the fora of Sbeilta *(Sufetula)*, Bulla Regia and Dougga.

The winter baths, covering 1,600 square metres and the summer baths, covering 2,400 square metres constitute the largest thermal complex and one of the most important monuments of the city. The baths date back to the late 2nd or early 3rd century A.D.

The palaestra of
Petronii.

A detail of a
geometric mosaic.

View of the theatre.

DOUGGA

Judging by the remains, *Thugga* is the most important ancient city in north-west Tunisia. It covers about 25 hectares and is situated on a hillside, from 500 to 600 metres in altitude. A Numidian city known as TBGG, it was undoubtedly one of the royal residences during the reigns of Massinissa and Micipsa. Its romanisation was rapid, but not imposed. Thanks to the generosity of the Dougga notables the city quickly erected large public monuments in the Roman style. The city was proclaimed a *municipium* in 205 A.D., and in 261 it was promoted to the rank of colony.

A visit to the site may begin with the Theatre built in 168-169 A.D., which is still well preserved. The tiers laid out in a semi-circle can accommodate 3,500 spectators. There are two honour-boxes which flank the orchestra box. The back of the orchestra is reserved for movable seats for the important dignitaries. A wall pierced by niches separate the orchestra from the stage.

The building constitutes a magnificent example for research and the technical quality of Roman theatres in North Africa. But Dougga is primarily famous for its Capitol — a temple dedicated to Jupiter, Juno and Minerva and built in honour of emperors Marcus Aurelius and Lucius Verus. It was built in 166-169

The capitol.

A.D. and consists of a monumental staircase leading to a portico which precedes the *cella.* The monument stands out for its beauty and its excellent state of preservation. Access to the capitol is usually gained from the Winds Dial Square, a paved square occupying the heart of the public square. It is bordered on three sides by porticoes behind which stand the temple of Mercury, the market and the temple of Fortuna. To the west it is dominated by the capitol. A large dial featuring the limits and centre of every one of the twelve winds, and their name, is engraved on the north-western part of the pavement.

The temple of Caelestis was built in the first three decades of the 3rd century A.D., during the reign of Septimus Severus. The temple stands in the centre of a closed semi-circular courtyard and is bordered by a portico of the same form. The temple to Juno Caelestis is built on a podium fronted by eleven steps. The *cella* is entirely surrounded by columns in the Corinthian style.

The Licinian baths (3rd century A.D.) are a large thermal installation parts of which suited the particularities of the bathers of the period. These include

View of the Licinian baths.

Dar El Acheb (Roman temple).

a *palestra* for wrestling exercises, changing rooms and warming up, wet and dry steam rooms for sweating, three *caldaria* (hot rooms) a *tepidarium* (tepid room) and a *frigidarium*.

Besides this large thermal complex, the city of Dougga has additional public thermal baths, (Baths of Aïn Doura) and the private baths of the Cyclops. The houses are built in the Mediterranean style, again encountered in the Arab-Moslem medinas. The privacy of the house is preserved by means of an entrance and gallery which formed an angle. The various rooms are built round a peristyle courtyard, the centre of which is sometimes embellished with an interior garden. The houses often include a first floor, reached from the outside by means of an elevated street, and which sometimes communicated with the ground floor by means of a staircase. The paving is adorned with beautiful mosaics such as those of the House of Dionysos and Ulysses and the House of Trifolium.

Dougga is a rare site, and it includes an extraordinary monument dating back to the Libyco-Punic civilisation (first half of 2nd century B.C.), namely a 20 m high mausoleum erected on square ground. A five step pedestal supports three floors, topped by a small pyramid. The walls of each floor feature a series of decorations, pillars with aeolian capitals, ionic columns, egyptian grooves, statues of a winged woman, a lion, etc. This masterpiece of Numidian royal architecture was the work of a native Lybic as is borne out by the commemorative inscription on the monument.

Also worth visiting on leaving the site is the Temple of Saturn dating back to 195 A.D. The temple stands on a holy site, the sanctuary of Baal, worshipped during the Punic period. The Roman temple was originally made up of an entrance with steps on top of which an interior porch with two columns was built and a paved area which was surrounded on three sides by a portico. At the back were three *cellae* reserved for the statues of the deities.

The temple of Caelestis.

Ruins of the church.

MAKTAR

Situated in the southern region of the Tunisian High Tell, at an altitude of 1,000 m, the ancient *Mactaris* dates back to the 3rd century B.C. During the Punic period it was the capital of an administrative district, but it passed under the authority of the kings of Massyle in 145 B.C. It obtained the status of a colony in the Roman period (180 A.D.) and was deserted in the 11th century after Beni Hillal's invasion. The modern town of Maktar was built near the ancient site.

Visitors first pass the triumphal arch of Bab Al Ain before reaching the site. The arch is situated within the limits of the new town. A neighbouring gully contains a tophet, where sacrifices took place in honour of Baal Hammon. The remains of the walls of the Numidian town are still visible about 500 metres to the right. The megalithic tombs are also of the Libyc or Numidian tradition. The great baths in the east, built shortly before 200 A.D. are the most impressive monument on the site, and among the best preserved in Africa.

The two public squares *(fora)* are well preserved, especially the new square constructed in the 2nd century A.D. The paving of the latter is almost intact and is reached through a triumphal arch dating back to the reign of emperor Trajan (116 A.D.). The city also has a market where, according to the inscription, god Mercury watched over the merchants. The museum includes Libyc inscriptions and a beautiful collection of steles originating from the tophet and dedicated to Baal Hammon. The inhabitants of *Mactaris* worshipped Baal Hammon until the second century A.D. They were still writing in Punic when the city became a Roman colony.

Trajan's arch.

Le Krib (Mustis).

Ruins of the Byzantine fortress, Aïn Tounga.

The arch, Le Krib (Mustis).

Views of Testour.

TESTOUR

Its main street teems with vendors of delicious country bread, known as the *Tabouna* bread. Testour is famous for its great mosque. The mosque dates back to the first half of the 17th century. The southern facade of its minaret features a clock dial, without hands. These used to turn counter-clockwise, and it seems to be the only example of such a clock in the Islamic world decorating a minaret. This distinctive feature resembles Spanish church towers.

Some houses are built in the Andalusian style, with tiled roofs. The *Melouf,* Andalusian music, can be heard during an annual festival.

Views of Le Kef.

LE KEF

Le Kef, the ancient *Sicca Veneria* was famous in the Punic period for its temple to Astarte (identified with the Roman Venus), goddess of fertility. The Punic city served as a rallying point for the mercenaries. Their rebellion was to prove costly to the Carthagian metropolis (240-237 B.C.). Some scattered remains date back to the Roman period, including remains of large baths, cisterns, Christian basilicas and remains of fortifications. The Kasbah constructed by the Arabs and rebuilt by the Turks in 1679 is the most beautifully preserved monument in Le Kef city. The Turkish fortress features defensive architecture. Several Arab monuments are also of interest, especially the Zawiya of Sidi Mizouni, built in 1834, with its large central cupola surrounded by four smaller cupolas, and the Mosque of Sidi Bou Makhlouf with an octagonal minaret flanked by two ribbed cupolas. The Zawiya of Sidi Ben Aissa (1784) is also a small regional museum of folk art and traditions. Exhibits include collections of costumes, jewels, pottery and other accessories of the horseman's dress in this captivating Tellian region.

THE CAP-BON REGION

Situated near Tunis the Cap-Bon region has developed into one of the most popular tourist resorts in Tunisia with Hammamet and Nabeul considered to be the ''Tunisian Riviera''. Cap-Bon is a vast orchard of citrus fruit. P1 motorway leads directly to Hammamet. Alternatively one may choose to take a right turn to Soliman to visit Hammam-Lif and Korbous.

Hammam-Lif, the small town of Naro has flourished since the Punic period. Situated at the foot of Bou Kornine, a holy mountain, venerated first as Baal's and then as Saturn's sanctuary, it has witnessed the history of Tunisia since Elyssa's landing. Under the Romans, the site was known as *Aquae Persianae*. It is now known as Hammam El Enf or Hammam-Lif, (derived from its French name).

The small resort flourished after the construction of a pavilion by the bey of Tunis, who wished to enjoy its thermal waters. Hammam-Lif became one of the summer residences of the beys.

The Bou Kornine heights offer a magnificent view of the Gulf of Tunis.

From Hammam-Lif one may continue to Korbous, a small thermal station known as *Aquae Caledae Carpitanae* in the Roman period. It has taken its current name from Sidi Al Karbanti, a holy man native of this city.

It was revived during the reign of Ahmed Bey (1837-1855) who built a pavilion, and established Korbous as one of Tunisia's most visited sites, a reputation it continues to enjoy. Korbous is set in beautiful landscape, and has different springs: Al-Kebira (the big spring), Ech-Cheffa (health), and Es-Sbia (the virgin), whose medicinal waters are used to treat rheumatism, skin and digestive problems. A modern hotel clinging to the mountain side, allows for an agreeable stay and a magnificent view of the Gulf of Tunis.

Korbous is also famous for its *Arraka*, a subterranean steam room, popular among those who seek to lose weight. Close by is Ain Oktor, a hydromineral station, with a hotel and water bottling plant, set within the wild countryside of Cap-Bon.

After Korbous the C26 road passes through Zaouit El Magaiz and leads to Sidi Daoud, well worth a visit. Known in antiquity as *Missua*, Sidi Daoud is famous among Tunisians for its first rate tinned tuna, used as a key ingredient in the traditional mechouia salad and eggbriks.

A short distance from Sidi Daoud is the village of El Haouaria. Two kilometres north-west of this village on the sea stand the famous ''caves'', essentially quarries which provided the sandstone used in the construction of Phoenician Carthage and many other coastal cities, among which Kerkouane. El Haouaria sandstone was also used in the Roman period.

During the first half of May it hosts the sparrow hawk festival. The bird of prey is captured and trained in this region to hunt quails and hares. El Haouaria and Sidi Daoud offer good views of Zembra island.

From El Haouaria on the C27 road is the Punic city of Kerkouane.

Some twelve kilometres from Kerkouane the road leads to Kelibia.

Famous for its beautiful beach, El Mansourah, Kelibia, remains despite its continuing expansion, a big village which is popular with visitors who taste grilled sardines or sip tea at the Port cafe in the afternoon and gaze out on the trawlers heading for the open sea, lighting up the water like beads of pearls.

Known in antiquity as *Aspis* or *Clupea*, the site was occupied by Agathocles in 310 B.C. and Regulus in 256 B.C. The fate of the city after the third Punic war was a tragic one. Little remains from the past. Worth visiting, however, are the Roman houses near the fishing school, and El Mansourah Punic necropolis. The main monument is the fortress which weathered the Spanish attacks of 1535 and 1547. Built atop a 150 m high rocky promontory the fortress stands guard over the Sicily Channel. Remains indicate that the strategic site was occupied since the Punic period. It has retained its military vocation since then.

From Kelibia towards Menzel Temime and Korba the road leads to Nabeul, which despite its proximity to Hammamet, has retained its distinctive charm, combining a beautiful beach with centuries old traditional crafts, notably those of ceramics and pottery.

A short distance from Nabeul is Hammamet.

Overall view of Hammamet.

HAMMAMET

This colourful city with its luxuriant vegetation, the vast sandy beaches, lined with hotels and luxurious villas, must be experienced to be believed.

The air of Hammamet is scented by mandarin and lemon blossom, jasmine and geraniums. The white-washed medina and the modern city stand out against the blue sea. The Medina is still surrounded by the ramparts recalling the years when the Spanish threat made them so imperative. Access is possible though a main gate, along an alley lined with shops which leads to an imposing Kasbah. This was built in the 15th century to replace a 12th century fort. During the protectorate, the Kasbah housed the Foreign Legion. The ramparts offer a splendid view of the Gulf of Hammamet, and allows for an in-

quisitive peep into the houses of Hammamet. The Kasbah now houses a museum dedicated to the ram. The International Cultural Centre, built on the magnificent property of the Rumanian multi-millionaire, George Sebastian, houses a theatre built in the style of an ancient theatre. In the summer, the town hosts a festival while in the winter it is a venue for numerous conferences. Tourism has boomed in this region since the first years of independence in the late 50s which has resulted in the construction of a large number of hotels, that have made Hammamet one of the most important tourist resorts in Tunisia.

Some of these hotels have been constructed over the ruins of the ancient city of *Pupput,* the remains of which can be seen south of the city, near Samira Club.

Views of the Medina.

Beach views of Hammamet.

Decorative ceramic tiles.

NABEUL

This distinctively charming town near Hammamet combines a beautiful beach with centuries old traditions, notably those of ceramics and pottery.

Besides the large factories, there are also a number of small workshops, producing fine crockery. The ceramics are exquisite, and their decoration is as fine as a painting.

Nabeul is also an important producer of perfume, especially orange and jasmine scents, and is famous for its fine embroidery.

The weekly market, every Friday, is a festive event. The market, one of the most important in Tunisia, spans traditional crafts and the latest hi-fi systems, bags of spices, and the famous brands of Paris perfumes. Even camels are on sale at times.

At the beginning of the main street leading to the sea is a newly built museum, with a fine collection of mosaics from Kerkouane and ceramics from Kelibia.

Also exhibited are the life-size terra-cottas from the country sanctuary of Thinissut. These represent the mother goddess, feeding her son and the lion headed goddesses, symbols of fertility.

Remains of the ancient Neapolis are found on the shore at the exit of the city, in the direction of Hammamet. The city was destroyed in 148 B.C. because it sided with Carthage. It reappeared under the Romans, in the late 3rd century A.D., obtaining the status of a colony.

Worth visiting on the site is the Roman industrial installation for the production of *garum*, a special fish sauce and salted fish. There is also a large house with more than twenty rooms covering 1,500 square metres which can be visited on this site. This house which dates back to the 4th century A.D. is called *Nympharum Domus*, the house of the Nymphs and its name is inscribed in the pool of the peristyle. Paving from the house is exhibited in the museum.

Decorative ceramic tiles.

The evergreen, growing out of a ceramic pot, considered to be the symbol of Nabeul.

Typical shop.

Ceramic tiled façade.

Roman statue of an emperor,
2nd to 3rd century A.D.

Statue of a seated goddess, 1st century A.D.

A mosaic depicting
the offering of
presents,
4th century A.D.

View of the interior
of the museum.

View of the remains of Kerkouane.

KERKOUANE

Founded in the 6th century B.C. Kerkouane was deserted in the mid 3rd century B.C., after it was sacked in 256 B.C. by Regulus. Built on the sea, the city is fortified on the northern, southern and western sides by a defensive system unique in the Phoenician-Punic world; there exist two walls each belonging to a different period, built of hard material and a superstructure in unfired bricks. The site also features several out buildings (two gates, towers, entrance, stairs and warehouses). Because Kerkouane was never occupied after its abandonment, it has remained a virgin Punic site, and is considered in ar-chaeological circles to be "the Punic Pompey". The city is well preserved and built in a regular pattern, with houses laid out in blocks, vast squares and beautiful homes with magnificent Punic paving of crushed ceramics adorned with white marble cubes, and equipped with impressive hip baths. The city had a large craft section, with workshops and shops, and a temple. The city of the dead extends on neighbouring cliffs. The Punic tombs are cut into the rock and include stairs, a short gallery and a funeral room, the walls of which often hold a multicoloured decoration. The necropolis of Arg el Ghazouani also deserves a short stop.

The most frequent type of residence in Kerkouane

is that of a house with a central courtyard. The entrance opens on to a passage forming an angle (designed to protect privacy), and on to a courtyard with a well and stairs leading to an upper room. The houses of Kerkouane are notable for the almost uniform presence of a bathroom, composed of a hip bath with a seat and arm rests, and sometimes equipped with a sink and water supply. The waste water and rain water were drained towards the courtyard by drains, linked to the central sewer. In some cases the courtyard is partly covered by porticoes, on one, two, three or even four sides, forming a peristyle courtyard resembling the Greek model.

The city also contains possibly the most important Punic sanctuary excavated to date. The monumental entrance of the sanctuary is flanked by two pilaster bases, and leads to a hall with seats on all four sides. At the end of the hall is a large courtyard, surrounded by several out buildings, among them a kiln, a workshop for statuettes, a bathroom and small yard used for storing clay. There is an altar in the courtyard, and at the far end two *podia,* facing east, each with a seat built of unfired bricks. The two *podia* belong to the chapels or the *cellae* of the holy place. Behind the *podia,* extends the rear of the yard. Originally built with one courtyard and one altar and only one *cella* or chapel in the centre, the sanctuary was later altered, and some annexes and the second podium were constructed.

The museum contains several collections, originating mainly from the necropolis. A small cell contains a beautiful wooden anthropoid sarcophagus its cover featuring a statue of a woman. This unique piece recalls the marble anthropoid sarcophagus found in Carthage. A glass case contains jewels toiletries and other articles used by women.

Also exhibited are some of the most beautiful ceramic pieces excavated at the site, including Punic pottery, and imported pottery, especially black glazed pottery. The Kerkouane pantheon is represented in a series of terra-cotta figurines of male and female deities, while objects of worship, such as incense burners, altars, and ostrich eggs are also exhibited.

Mosaic floor depicting the Punic symbol of Tanit.

View of Hammam-Lif.

Typical scenes of the Cap-Bon region.

View of Sidi Daoud.

*Overall view of
Korbous.*

*View of the fort of
Kelibia.*

THE SAHEL

The Sahel is the olive producing coastal area extending from Sousse in the north to Sfax in the south. Since independence the Sahel region has developed into one of the prime tourist areas in Tunisia without, however, neglecting its agriculture which has acclaimed itself the olive producing area of Tunisia concentrated mainly in the olive grove area around Sfax. Leaving Hammamet the P1 road leads to Enfida. From Enfida a right turn leads to Kairouan which has reigned supreme as Africa's first city of Islam since its foundation. A short distance from Kairouan is the Islamic museum of Raqqada. Alternatively, from Enfida P1 leads to Sousse the third largest city in Tunisia. Sousse with its historic Medina, its museum and its splendid tourist accommodation, has been undergoing a period of growth. A few kilometres to the north of Sousse is Port El Kantaoui, created by the authorities in the mid 1970s and considered to be the first Mediterranean "garden-port".

To the south of Sousse is Monastir which is also turning into a tourist resort with its airport situated close by. From Monastir the road continues towards Mahdia, the first capital of the Fatimid Dynasty.

The MC87 road leads from Mahdia to El Djem which can also be reached directly from Sousse on the P1 road.

The amphitheatre of El Djem is clearly visible to the visitor from a great distance, its silhouette standing out against a monotonous landscape, and looming large over a city of low, white houses, seemingly on their knees in front of this majestic monument. *Thysdrus,* was a modest Punic village in the 3rd century B.C. and in the early years after Christ. In order to punish it for its support to the Pompeyans, Caesar demanded a quantity of wheat, though only very small, from its inhabitants. Archaeological digs indicate that the city began to flourish in the 1st century A.D. This continued over into the next century, and the city reached its zenith during the late second and early third centuries A.D., when it gained the status of a municipality. In 238 its inhabitants rebelled against the central power, and proclaimed Gordianus the new emperor replacing the deposed Maximinus.

Gordianus was soon defeated. But for some time, Africa was to accommodate the capital of the Roman empire.

The expansion of *Thysdrus* in the Roman period is due to two factors — the olive tree and commerce. The city was at the crossroads of central Tunisia, and covered nearly 180 hectares. The surface of its ruins classifies it as one of the largest Roman cities in Africa, and in the entire Roman empire.

Apart from the amphitheatre *Thysdrus* boasts other monuments which can rival those of Rome. Thus, the circus, which has still to be excavated, was 550 m in length and 95 m in width and could accommodate 30,000 spectators, equal to Maxence's circus in Rome.

The houses, real palaces, are among the largest and most luxurious in North Africa. The houses could be as large as 3,000 square metres, and included an imposing main body and a complex of secondary apartments and annexes, of greater or lesser importance. The town's museum features an impressive collection of mosaics, works of the school of Byzacera so exquisite that they resemble tapestry work.

From El Djem the P1 road leads to Sfax. Even though Sfax has not seen the touristic development characteristic of other coastal cities in Tunisia, it still constitutes a necessary stop on the way south. Famous for the sea of olive tree groves that surround it, Sfax is also an industrial city, and an important harbour. It is also the leading market for octopus and sponges in Tunisia.

THE ISLAMIC MUSEUM OF RAQQADA

Raqqada, 9 km south of Kairouan, originally founded by Ibrahim Ibn Al Aghlab in 876 in order to enjoy a ''gay life'' away from inquisitive eyes, is now the site of a museum of Islamic art.

Situated within the ancient presidential palace, the museum features the most famous collection of parchments in the Islamic world. The parchment is made of treated skin of goat, sheep or more rarely gazelle, and used as writing material. It also features pages of the blue Koran, written in golden Kufi (a style of Arabic) and a model of the Kairouan grand mosque. The numismatic department offers a wealth of information on Tunisian history during the Islamic period.

Some of the exhibits of the museum.

*The minaret
of the Great
Mosque.*

KAIROUAN

Kairouan, or more precisely Al Kayrawan, was founded by Okba Ibn Nafaa with the specific aim of perpetuating the glory of Islam until the end of time. His wish seems to have been granted.

Founded in 671 A.D. by Okba, Kairouan combines monuments of historical and religious importance with a population deeply rooted in the traditions of Arab-Moslem culture.

The Great Mosque, or Jamaa Sidi Okba, the oldest religious monument of western Islam, is the city's pride. The monument, 135 metres in length and 80 metres in width, is famous for its squat massive minaret with its three square platforms diminishing in size and crowned with a cupola. The mihrab, inside the prayer room, is surrounded by metal-lustre glazed tiles imported from Baghdad in the 9th century. The pulpit or minbar, from which the Imam pronounces his weekly sermon every Friday is made from carved wooden panels dating back to the Ibrahim Ibn Ali Aghlab period.

A model of this mosque can be seen in the Raqqada Islamic Museum. Other than for a few details, the mosque has retained its present form since the 9th century. At the time, Kairouan was, along with Medine in Arabia and Kufa in Iraq, one of the main centres of Islam.

Kairouan is also the site of the reservoir of the Aghlabids, and is flanked by a basin.

This reservoir, a 48 side polygon with a total diametre of 128 metres, received the waters of Jebel Cherichera, 36 kilometres away, via an aqueduct. Water also flowed into a smaller reservoir, a 17 side polygon with a diametre of 37.40 m. Thanks to this reservoir, the emirs of the Aghlabid could combine work with pleasure. A square pillar in the centre of the reservoir undoubtedly supported a pavilion where the emir could rest.

Among the zaouia, a visit to Sidi Sahab is essential. Abu Zamaa el Balawi, venerated as the Prophet's barber because he kept three hairs from the

One of the gates of the Medina.

Prophet's beard, was in fact one of his faithful companions. This zaouia which was altered several times is famous for its magnificent wooden ceilings. The mausoleum cupola was built in 1629, the minaret and medersa in 1685-1690. The Medina, surrounded by a three kilometre long rampart, with battlements flanked by several round buttresses criss-crossed by a series of narrow winding streets, retains the charm of the past. It is also the site of a large number of important monuments: Bir Barouta with its famous noria, the zaoura of Sidi Abid El Ghariani, the three door mosque founded by an Andalusian from Cordoba in 866 among them.

The Three Doors Mosque.

View of the ribbed dome of the Great Mosque.

Craftsmen at work in Kairouan.

Kairouan also represents tradition. The *makroudh*, a cake baked in this city, has long been famous. These small diamond shaped cakes are made from pastry, stuffed with dates and dipped in honey. Kairouan rugs are famous well beyond Tunisia's borders. During the religious feasts, both Tunisian and foreign visitors converge on the city. The nights of the fasting month of Ramadan are unforgettable. *Mouled*, the Prophet's birthday is celebrated with particular splendour. These religious feasts are often accompanied by circumcision ceremonies, organised for hundreds of boys in Sidi Saheb's Mausoleum.

Views of the souks of Kairouan.

Waterwheel of Bir Barouta.

Overall view of Sousse.

SOUSSE

A city with a thousand names, among them *Adrim, Hadrumetum, Hunericopolis, Justinianopolis,* Sousse is the pearl of the Sahel, combining the most beautiful faces of ancient and modern Tunisia. Founded by the Phoenicians, after Utica and Carthage, probably in the 8th century B.C., the city sided with Rome in 149 B.C. at the time of the third Punic war, thus protecting itsel from the risks of war. A colony under Trajan (98-117A.D.), it exported cereals and olive oil from its hinterland to Rome and the Orient. Under Diocletian (284-305) it became the capital of the new province of Byzacena. In the 5th century A.D., the Vandals named the city *Hunericopolis* after Huneric, their chief's son. The Byzantines renamed it *Justinianopolis* in the 6th century, after Emperor Justinian. With the Islamic conquest it was renamed Sousse, a name it has retained.

The golden age of Islamic Sousse was in the 9th century A.D., during the reign of Aghlabid, when it served as the harbour of the capital Kairouan. The Ribat, the main monument of the city, dates back to that period. Sousse was annexed by the Normands after the Hilalian invasion, and was liberated by the Almohadi, who had come from Morocco in 1160. In the 17th century it became a pirate's den. The city was bombed during the Second World War (1942-43). Although traces of the ancient *Hadrumetum* have in the most part disappeared, those dating back to the Aghlabid period still remain

The Ribat.

View of the fortifications.

View of a room with mosaics.

Mosaic depicting God Ocean, 2nd century A.D.

Mosaic depicting the head of Gorgo, 2nd century A.D.

intact. Only the catacombs and the museum collection remain from the Roman period. The catacombs of ancient *Hadrumetum* were used from the late 2nd to the late 3rd centuries A.D.

More than 5 km long, they are made up of 240 galleries grouping some 15,000 burials in four distinctive groups.

Three of these were excavated, and bear the name of Hermes, Severus and Good Shepherd. The inscriptions and funeral accessories are exhibited in the museum of the city.

The ribat of Sousse is among the most famous monuments of the city. Built in the late 8th century, the Aghlabid Emir Ziyadet Allah I added a tower in 821. With its semi-cylindrical towers in the corners, and in the middle of the sides, the ribat's first floor has a prayer room which occupies all the southern wing. Facing the ribat is another historic monument, the Great Mosque, built probably in 851 by the Aghlabid Emir Abu Al Abbas Mohammed. This mosque resembles a fortress. The Medina deserves particular attention. The gates of the Medina remain intact. A walk along the axis Bab al Jedid (the new gate) and Bab el Gharbi (the western or sunset gate) will reveal how this oriental town has managed to retain its traditions in the narrow souks, brimming with people.

The kasbah of Sousse overlooks the Medina, and commands the landscape with is famous tower, named after its designer, Khalaf Al Fata. This thirty metre high tower served previously as a signals tower, and now operates as a lighthouse. Erected in 859, the kasbah has been reconstructed several times in the period between the 11th and 15th centuries.

The kasbah also houses the museum. The latter includes a very rich collection of mosaics, masterpieces produced by the mosaic schools of the region. Of special note is a mosaic representing the triumph of Bacchus. Discovered near the small Sahelian village of Smirat (Amira), it depicts amphitheatre games and gladiators and is of extreme historical importance.

Part of the interior of the museum.

The museum also houses some steles of the Phoenico-Punic period. They come from the tophet, where the tutelary deity is only Baal Hammon.

But there is more than history. The esplanade of Bou Jaafer running parallel to the beach of the same name, is one of the most beautiful sights of the city, and of the country. Sousse is also an important tourist resort, with scores of hotels.

Sousse also retains the traditions of the past. The feast of Aoussou, has continued to be celebrated here in late July. The feast dates back to the Roman homage to Neptune, and people still move to the sea, staying up late to bathe in order to rid their bodies of pain. The weekly market of Sousse is the meeting place for the entire Tunisian Sahel.

Mosaic depicting "Ichtus", late 3rd century A.D.

Sousse: view of the beach.

Sousse: views of the beach.

The golf course and overall view of Port El Kantaoui.

PORT EL KANTAOUI

Port of El Kantaoui is one of the most famous marinas in the Mediteranean. Buildings within this marina are built in the architectural style of Sidi Bou Said, and include a large number of cafes, restaurants, boutiques, a genuine souk. Nearby is an 18 hole golf course and other sports facilities, helping to make it a veritable mecca for summer visitors.

The entrance to Port El Kantaoui.

Overall view of Monastir.

MONASTIR

Several tombs dug in Sidi Al Ghedamsi island (now shapeless caves) indicate that this area was settled long before the Punic period. However, the present city of Monastir was not built on the site of the Punico-Roman city of *Ruspina,* but several kilometres to the south-east, in Henchir Tenir, over looking the *sebkha.* It is here that Caesar set up camp during his famous war against Pompey in 49-46 B.C. And it was here that during the Islamic conquest, the special envoy of the Abbassid caliph Haroun Al Rashid, Harthama Ibn Ayun, built the first ribat of Tunisia in 796.

Monastir's wide open spaces make it different from other Tunisian cities. Only the main buildings stand-out against the blue horizon.

The ribat, the first such fortification to be built in the country and the model for the construction of other ribats, is imposingly large. In the 9th and 11th centuries, the initial level was embodied within more powerful fortifications. Its round tower offers a view of the entire city. A small Islamic arts museum is found in one of the monument's wings.

In front of the ribat is the Great Mosque, built in the 9th century and then rebuilt in the eleventh. The Great Mosque played a double role of fortress and sanctuary, and the fact that it does not have a minaret gives it the appearance of a simple fortification.

Most striking among the modern buildings is the beautiful Bourguiba Mosque, built in 1963. Close by is the Bourguiba family mausoleum, which can be recognised by its two 25 metre high minarets flanking a golden cupola. It is fronted by a magnificent esplanade with two octagonal pavilions. The adjacent cemetery contains the mausoleum of Sidi el Mezri, (12th century), a native of Mazzara del Vallo in Sicily, and as local folklore notes, a great patron of the city.

The growing number of hotels, the marina, next to the ribat, the golf course, sited on the remains of ancient *Ruspina,* the international airport, the museum of folk art and traditions, the international festival and the serene environment have made Monastir an excellent tourist resort and an ideal stage point from which to discover the small, bustling villages of the Tunisian Sahel, and the nearby Kuriate islands.

View of the Ribat.   *Coastal view of Monastir.*

The Skifa el Kahla (dark porch).

MAHDIA

Madhia, the first capital of the Fatimid dynasty is situated on a rocky peninsula, 1,500 m in length and less than 500 m in width, tapering off as Cap Africa and linked to the continent by a narrow isthmus. Obeid Allah el Mahdi, founder of the Fatimid dynasty, (Shiite Moslems) built the city in 916 and settled there in 921. Mahdia remained the capital until 947-948 when Al Mansour transferred the government headquarters to Sabra, a newly built city, situated close to Kairouan. Its strategic position made Mahdia an important base for the pirates and explains its eventful history. The city was occupied by Roger of Sicily from 1148 to 1160. Charles V occupied it for three years, before destroying its fortifications and abandoning it in 1554. However, contrary to popular belief, human settlement of the area dates back to the Punic period, and the peninsula was in fact one of the necropolis of the Punic city of *Gumi*, probably located at the entrance of the isthmus. Mahdia is famous for its Skifa el Kahla (dark porch) *The Great Mosque.*

that is, the new entrance of the old city, built after the destruction of the old fortifications during the Spaniards retreat in 1554.

The new ramparts included small forts and artillery platforms, and the Skifa pierces one of these small forts.

During the weekly markets, the Skifa is transformed into a veritable scene from One Thousand and One Nights, where women sell beautiful traditional costumes and gold jewels.

The Great Mosque of Mahdia, as the first mosque to be built by the Shiites in 921 has also earned a special place in Moslem religious architecture. The mosque does not have a minaret. It originally had a monumental door dedicated to the Mahdi and initially shared two walls with ramparts. During the Spanish occupation, its oratory was transformed into a church, which was destroyed during the retreat. During the 1960's (1961-65) the mosque was faithfully reconstructed along the lines of the original 10th century plan.

A visit to Borj El Khebir offers a splendid view of both the Mediterranean and Sahel coasts. Built in the 16th century, but featuring bastions more reminiscent of the 18th century, the largely restored fortifications overlook the peninsula. Parts of the seaside rampart are still visible at its foot, while the interior port, cut out of the rocks in the Punic fashion, still shelters some small fishing boats.

Mahdia has all the charm characteristic of a coastal city. Its harbour cafes are open round the clock as fishermen do not keep a regular working schedule. The fish is sold at cheap prices on the quays, before it even reaches the market.

Along the boulevard surrounding the peninsula, hundreds of octopi are strung out to dry on terrace ropes. During October fishermen can be admired pursuing shoals of small mullet in their small boats.

And, besides the city's many charms, Mahdia also boasts some beautiful beaches.

The amphitheatre of El Djem.

EL DJEM

The amphitheatre or coliseum has, and will continue to make, this city famous. The date of its construction is still unknown, but probably goes back to the late 2nd or early 3rd century A.D.

The coliseum has a perimetre of 427 m, and its two axis are 148 and 122 m respectively, while those of the area are 64 and 39 m. The façade has three floors with 64 arcades, each crowned with a fourth floor. The amphitheatre is considered among the last important monuments of its kind to be built in the Roman empire and could accommodate 27,000 spectators. The coliseums of Rome and Carthage could accommodate 43,000 and 35,000 spectators respectively. El Djem thus ranks third among the amphitheatres of the empire, from the point of view of capacity along with the coliseum of Verona in Italy, but before those of Arles and Nîmes in France.

Access to the coliseum was easy, and allowed spectators to enter the premises within few minutes, and the work that went into this is finer than anywhere else.

After the Roman period, the coliseum served as an insurrectionary centre almost on a permanent basis. The Kahena, a Berber princess turned it into a fortress to fight the Islamic conquest, hence El Djem's other name, the Kahena's castle *(ksar)*.

Tribes rebelling against the fiscal policies of Tunis Beys were to take refuge there all the time and the authorities used cannon fire to render it unusable.

Views of the interior of El Djem.

View of the ramparts of the Medina.

SFAX

Very little is known about the ancient history of Sfax other than its name: *Taparura*. During the Islamic period the city did not flourish in the way that other cities such as Sousse or Mahdia did. Its relative prosperity goes back to the Aghlabid period. In 1881 the city was shelled before succumbing to the French protectorate. The city was bombed again during the Second World War (1942-43), and part of it was reconstructed.

Worth visiting are the souks of the Medina, which one enters through Bab Divan, a triple arched gate built in 1306, and the Great Mosque, constructed in 849. This three storey minaret is reminiscent of the Great Mosque in Kairouan. Dar Jallouli (the house of a famous Sfaxian family which has branches in Tunis) dates back to the 17th century and houses the regional museum of popular arts and customs. Visitors experience the life of Sfax and of the Sfaxians of the past, beginning with the kitchen complete with utensils and spices, and ending with a display of rich Sfaxian costumes and jewels.

The modern city bustles with bicycles and motor-cycles, more characteristic of cities of the Far East. The archaeological museum, situated within the municipality building, features a collection of finds, including Roman, pagan, and Christian mosaics, ceramics and glass, and shed a light on the history of the region, notably about Thaenas site (Henchir Thina) where most of the finds were excavated.

Bab Al-Divan.

The inner courtyard of the museum of popular arts and customs (Dar Jallouli).

The municipality.

Typical views of the Sahel.

View of an oasis.

SOUTHERN TUNISIA

The southern region presents the picture most easily associated with Tunisia. Travelling south, the steppe zone gives way to the desert. The northern part of the desert which is described here is easily accessible by road while a visit further south should only be attempted with a 4 wheel drive car or with a guided tour.

A visit to the desert and the oases with their tens of thousands of palm trees and camels is a unique opportunity for the visitor to experience a completely different way of life. Tozeur, Nefta, Kebili and Douz are a few of these oases which have developed into towns or villages and are located around the Chott el Djerid, the largest of the Sahara salt lakes with an area of almost 2,000 square km. In the western part of southern Tunisia is Gabes and further to the southern are the Berber settlements with their *ksars* and *ghorfas*, notably Medenine, Metameur and Chenini. A *ghorfa* is a long rectangular room with an arched ceiling which serves as a granary. Several *ghorfas* built round a courtyard form a *ksar*.

The coast of southern Tunisia is a unique sight with its endless sandy beaches lined with palm trees.

As southern Tunisia is very large it can be divided into an eastern and western region. The P3 road leads from Tunis to the eastern region and passes close to Kairouan from which the P3E road leads to the Roman site of Sbeitla, well worth a visit. From Sbeitla the P13 road leads to Kasserine via Feriana or alternatively one may reach Gafsa by taking the P13 towards an easterly direction and then the P3. From Gafsa the P3 leads to the oasis towns of Tozeur and Nefta. From Tozeur the P16 passes through the Chott el Djerid (salt lake) on to the oasis town of Kebili. From Kebili one may tour the eastern region by taking the P16 up to Gabes. From Gabes the MC107 leads to the troglodites of Matmata. Alternatively from Gabes the P1 leads to the *ksars* of Metameur and Medenine. South of Medenine is the Berber village of Chenini. To reach the island of Djerba from Medenine the shortest way is via the MC108 to Djorf through the Roman site of Gightis. From Djorf there is a ferry service to Ajim in Djerba. Alternatively from Medenine one can continue to Zarzis which is fast developing into a popular tourist resort and then along the coastal road which leads to the road that links the mainland with El Kantara in Djerba.

The capitol.

monumental gate, preceded by four steps. The gate is made up of a triple door arch, bearing an inscription dedicated to Antonin the Pious and dating back to 139 A.D. The forum is entirely surrounded by a 70 by 67 metre wall. The square, measuring 37.20 m in length and 34.75 in width is surrounded by porticoes on all but one of its sides. Three temples, making up the capitol and dedicated to Jupiter, Juno and Minerva stand impressively at the back. The three *cellae,* usually dedicated to each deity within one monument, are replaced in *Sufetula* by three temples. The monuments are separated at the base by three passages. A platform joins them at the floor, creating a tribune. *Sufetula* was also the eloquent testament of Christianity in ancient Tunisia and had at least 7 Christian monuments. The chapel of Jucundus, bears the name of a bishop martyred by the Vandals in the first half of the 5th century, and houses an impressive baptistry.

There are two other churches nearby that of Vitalis, founded in the 5th century and that of Bellator, founded in the 4th.

The ecclesiastical tour continues with the church of Servus, dedicated to the Saints Gervasius, Protasius and Tryphon, the basilica of the Saints Sylvanus and Fortunatus, and the chapel of the Bishop Honorius. Another characteristic of the city is its regular street plan. Streets intersect at right angles, and delimit blocks of houses facing in the same direction. This dates back to the late first or early second centuries A.D.

The city also boasts two Roman monuments — the Tetrarchy arch, a monumental gate with a 5.60 m span built around 300 A.D. and the bridge-aqueduct. The latter is 50 metres long and provides the city with water.

The recently constructed antiquarium of Sbeitla, houses a beautiful display of Roman ceramics dating from the 2nd to the 7th centuries A.D., funeral steles, sculptures from the Roman period as well as an Islamic section, featuring about 50 golden and silver coins of the 12th and 13th centuries.

View of the monumental gate and capitol.

SBEITLA (SUFETULA)

Sbeitla *(Sufetula),* originally Libyc, was unknown to ancient historians. Even its history in the Roman period remains obscure. The city emerged in the Byzantine period when the patrician Gregory proclaimed himself emperor, rejecting the authority of Basilius. A year later, Abdallah Ibn Saad at the head of Moslem troops put an end to this adventure. The patrician was killed and the city pillaged.

Sufetula's forum and capitol make it a key attraction. Access to the forum is gained through a

The ''Roman pool''.

GAFSA

Gafsa is one of the most ancient cities of Tunisia, and, was, according to tradition, founded by the illustrious Hercules. The region has been inhabited since the Paleolithic period and gave its name to a prehistoric civilisation, the Capsian civilisation. Gafsa constitutes for the prehistoric period what Carthage constituted for antiquity. The city is particularly famous for its ''Roman pool''. Made up of two pools, this is in fact a water temple dating back to the Roman period. It was built around the springs which are the reason for the town's foundation. This temple was protected by Neptune and the Nymphs.

The kasbah of Gafsa is also well worth a visit. Its imposing walls, with their quadrangular turrets and semi-circular towers were to some extent built from material taken from Roman constructions.

View of the walls of the kasbah.

Two typical views of Tozeur.

TOZEUR

The ancient city of *Thusuros* was a real garrison-town, built on the Roman limes (frontier), at the southern limit of the Province of Africa. Tozeur, the capital of the Jerid stands out against the whiteness of the *Chott* with its sand coloured houses. These are built with dry bricks arranged in such a way that they resemble the beautiful geometric reliefs of the ornamental tissues of the south. Tozeur is also an immense oasis, irrigated by 200 springs, its source of life. The water is distributed fairly on the basis of a system established in the 13th century by Ibn Chabbat.

The Belvedere offers a majestic view of the surroundings. Palm groves and date palms challenge the dry soil and climate; water from the inexhaustible springs flows through a vast number of paths and irrigation channels; the *Chott* with its white layers and troublesome mirages, and in the background, the glistening infinite horizon of the Sahara. Once in Tozeur, do not hesitate to discover ''Paradise'' a real Garden of Eden with its dazzling richly coloured flowers and a luxuriant variety of fruit trees. Tunisia's greatest poet Abu Al Kacem Ech Chabi, was not surprisingly, born in this fertile environment.

View of the Corbeille.

NEFTA

Another capitivating city of the Chott el Jerid, *Ag-gasel Nepte,* was originally built on the southern limes or frontier of the Roman province of Africa. Few traces of it remain.

The inhabitants of Nefta, like all the people of the south, were good Christians and once converted to the religion of the Prophet fervent defenders of Islam. Nefta still retains its religious vocation to the present day, and with one hundred marabouts and twenty four mosques, eight of which celebrate Friday prayers, it is considered to be an important religious centre of Tunisia.

The city's architecture is typical of the Jerid. The houses are of dry brick and present an authentically constructed tapestry whose artist has drawn from a very original iconographic collection. White cupolas tower over some houses brightening up the mass of clay-coloured buildings like flowers. One of the most beautiful oases of the Jerid is to be found here and fruit trees and vegetables grow in the shade of the palm trees. The palm groves are irrigated by 152 springs. From the Sahara Palace one can look over into the Corbeille of Nefta. This masterpiece of nature is a hollow flanked by abrupt cliffs overlooking a dark, cool grove which shelters a beautiful orchard, a veritable spring of life in a landscape at war with the sand dunes.

Typical scenes of
South-eastern
Tunisia.

Typical scenes of South-eastern Tunisia.

Two views of the oasis of Gabes.

GABES

The city of Sidi Boulbaba presents a unique landscape — an oasis extending on the Syrtes Gulf shore and combines the verdant beauty of an oasis with ochre coloured sandy beaches and the azure blue waters of the Mediterranean.

Gabes was an ancient Punic harbour, which became a Roman colony under the name of *Tacapa.* Under the banner of Islam, Gabes has known a glorious destiny, becoming a stronghold fortified with ramparts and ditches which were flooded in case of need, a real fortress dominating all the south of Ifriqiya.

Gabes is worth a stop-over whatever the nature of the tour of southern Tunisia. The Sidi Boulbaba Mosque contains the tomb of the Prophet's barber who settled in Gabes in the 7th century. The tomb constitutes a holy place for Moslems. The folk arts and traditions museum is to be found in the old medina. The oasis merits a ride in an open carriage where Pliny the Elder's testimony on the richness of cultivation flourishing in the shade of the palm trees still holds true.

Exhibits of the folk arts and traditions museum, Gabes.

Views of Matmata.

THE LAND OF MATMATA

The Jebel Demer is an arid mountainous arch in southern Tunisia. The mountains border on the desert and are the home of a number of tribes, holding on tenaciously in the face of a range of natural and other dangers. The cave dwelling villages perch on the mountain crests, below the *ksours*. These impregnable and unchanging granaries defy time. The *ksar*, made up of several *ghorfas* is an imposing collective granary overhanging the mountains. It is difficult to distinguish the entrance of the mud-coloured dwellings. The crests of the Jebel Demer are rocky, and its many craters give it almost a lunar landscape. The Land of Matmata is famous for its cave dwellings, situated within immense craters. A lateral tunnel which can be closed by a palm-tree wood door,

leads to a large open courtyard 10 metres in diametre and 6 to 7 metres in height. The rooms, some of which are large, and other annexes are to be found around this yard. Rooms on the first floor are often used for storage and can be reached by means of either some rudimentary steps or a rope. The olive presses of the village are also carved into the rock and rely on archaic equipment. The dwellings are cool in the summer and warm in the winter.

The cave dwellings of Matmata.

The landscape near Chenini.

CHENINI

Chenini is a Berber village whose beauty and charm is jealously hidden under the folds of the terrain. The only thing visible of this subterranean town is the imposing silhouette of the *ksar* over hanging the crest of Chenini. This is a large loft-citadel, the *ghorfas* of which in the past served as a granary and as the

The village of Chenini.

Metameur.

Two views of the ksars of Medenine.

ultimate refuge for the co-owners, in the event of an invasion. Below, the dwellings of the village are carved into the rock face, under the mountain slopes. This Berber village also has an ancient mosque. Its minaret seems to watch over the giant tombs of the Seven Sleepers, personalities of a legend known in several regions of Tunisia.

Chenini caves are cut into two parts. The first series of 7 to 8 metres long by 2 metres high and 3 to 4 metres wide, are used as a home. They adjoin a second excavation, of 4 to 5 metres long, which is used for storage. The caves become bigger parallel to the mountain side, as the needs of the families for space increase. The yard is situated in front of the gate on a floor protected by a wall securing the privacy of the space reserved for the daily activities of women. Sunset at Chenini village is especially captivating, and made all the more so by the commotion created by the women preparing dinner in the courtyard.

THE KSOURS OF MEDENINE

The collective granary of Medenine is an example of the *ksars* in the plains. The origin of the *ksars* is a collection of several *ksars* from different communities grouped in more than 25 courtyards, with as many as 6,000 *ghorfas* piled up on four or five layers. This huge collective granary was carefully guarded. Unfortunately only a small number of *ghorfas*, arranged around two courtyards remain. The *ghorfa* is a small oblong cell, 4 to 5 metres deep, two metres high and two metres wide. The door is located in one of the two extremities. Because of the scarcity of building materials for the framework, the *ghorfa* is covered by a ribbed vault built of stones and lime. From the outside, and because of the absence of an opening the *ksar* has the appearance of a solid rampart.

ZARZIS

Zarzis is a small coastal town of the south, formerly known as *Gergis*. The white mass of its typical houses and public buildings stand out clearly against the olive tree and palm groves, on the one hand, and the blue horizon on the other. Zarzis is also a busy fishing harbour and has a small local museum. The partly excavated ancient site of Ziane is situated some 10 kilometres away.

Zarzis remains a charming resort in the middle of the desert, offering both the pleasures of the sea and the serenity of the south.

Views near Zarzis.

*Sunrise near
Zarzis.*

GIGHTIS

Situated at the far end of Bou Grara Gulf, Gightis was a prosperous harbour of the Syrtes. Ships would be loaded with the goods brought by caravan across the Sahara. Gightis was also a port of call for ships coming from the Orient, Magna Grecia, Egypt and Tripolitania. In 202 B.C. this large Carthaginian harbour passed under the rule of the Numidian king, Massinissa who had annexed the Emporia. From 46 B.C. onwards when it became a part of the Roman empire, the city flourished further, reaching its zenith. Following the Vandal invasion the site was progressively abandoned.

The remains depict the glorious past of what was once a great Roman city. Several public buildings still remain, among them the forum, baths, the capitol, the market, a civil basilica and several temples dedicated to different deities of the Roman pantheon.

The ruins of Gightis.

The fortress of Borj el Kebir (Great Fort), Houmt Souk.

DJERBA

The beauty of this Mediterrranean island is legendary. Homer vaunts the bewitching virtues of the land of the lotos eaters in the Odyssey, writing, ''as soon as one of Ulysses' envoys tastes these honey fruits, he no longer wants to go home or to send his news''. Ulysses was obliged to seize them by force, put them in chains and hasten the departure for fear of postponing for ever the date of their return home. The atmosphere is still filled with the scent of this mysterious lotos flower, and continues to bewitch every visitor to the island. Visitors will not need to throw a coin in a fountain of water in order to return to Djerba. A mysterious thread links them for ever.

The homeric legend symbolises the charming beauty of the island, its belts of palm trees, its luxurious gardens full of fruit trees, its typical dwellings *(menzels)*, its mosques with their characteristic minarets, its solid fortresses, testifying to the eventful history of this strategic island, coveted by Mediterranean forces from time immemorial. Its extensive beaches, with their fine silvery sand, and their quiet and intimate character, notwithstanding the rapid and intense arrival of tourism.

Ancient historiography of the Phoenico-Punic period refers to the island's famous purple dye, obtained from the murex shell. The remains of a Lybico Punic mausoleum of Henchir Bourgou, a royal tomb, dates back to that period. Visible too are some remains

Loading pottery in Houmt Souk.

from the famous ancient *Meninx* (El Kantara). The name place of the island can be traced back several centuries, thanks to the inscription *Ghirba* found in Houmt Souk and dating back to the 3rd century B.C. In view of its strategic position, the island has lived through significant historical events since the Arab conquest. It was the stage for a series of invasions and battles waged against Byzantium by the kings of Sicily and Spain, especially the major expedition of Philip II, in 1560. Its strategic position also led to a similar involvement in the course of the pirate attacks.

Djerba is a flat island, with a Saharan climate tempered by the influence of the sea. It covers 514 square kilometres, and its coastline spans 125 kilometres. It is inhabited by the Berbers, who have preserved their native language (the Berber dialect is still spoken) and their regional characteristics. Converted to Islam, the inhabitants of Djerba soon declared themselves the followers of the Kharijite sect, a sect considered schismatic by Sunni Orthodox moslems. The extreme piety of the Djerbians is reflected in the large number of mosques in proportion to the size of the island, and some claim that there are 213 places of worship. The mosques share a characteristic style, with cupolas, vaults, and cylindrical minarets. Their simplicity and originality is of great beauty. Especially interesting among the mosques, is the Zawiya of Sidi Brahim el Jamni (1674-1702) the Mosque of the Foreigners, and the Turks mosque.

Villages such as Mahboubine, Midoun and Cedghiane have beautiful, well kept orchards, despite the scarcity of underground water on the island. It is characteristic of Djerba that houses are spread out; *menzels* are scattered all over the orchards, as are beautiful houses topped with cupolas in which privacy forms an integral part of the architectural plan. The fishing potential off the island's coasts is enormous, and fishing is carried out with nets, either with boats, or in fisheries. Lanes of palms *(zribas)* in the open sea help to direct considerable quantities of fish towards the harbour. The fish is still sold by auction.

Thanks to the National Office of Tourism and the private initiative of several businessmen, the island of Djerba has the necessary hotel infrastructure. The hotels are built along some of the most beautiful beaches of the island, with wide open spaces in between.

Visitors should not fail to visit Borj el Kebir (Borj Ghazi Mustapha) a fortress dating back to the 15th century.

Views of Houmt Souk.

The interior of the Ghriba.

The fortress dominates the sea, while each of its towers and fortifications tells the story of the many conquerors who succeeded each other, until the arrival of the Turks.

Djerba accommodates a Jewish community who first settled there is ancient times. Hara Kebira is a Jewish neighbourhood. Though very old, its synagogue is not well known. In another Jewish neighbourhood, Hara Sghira (Er Riadh) is the synagogue, the Ghriba. The Ghriba is a pilgrimage site and contains one of the oldest Torahs in the world. Noteworthy also is the fact that the synagogue's rabbi speak and write Judeo-Arabic, that is Arabic transcribed into Hebrew. This language is disappearing in North Africa. The rabbi reads the holy text in Hebrew, but explains and comments on Mosaic law to the faithful in Arabic. The horn sounds at sunset every Friday indicating the beginning of the Sabbath.

Guellala is a potter's village situated in the south of the island. Pottery is one of the art industries of the island, and craftsmen use the clay from the quarries to mould large jars, various utensils, among them the Djerbian couscous pots with two compartments, *(bou rouhine)*, small modelled pottery and glazed pottery. Despite the stiff competition from the industrial sector, Guellala craftsmen work hard to preserve their craft from a slow and painful death. Visitors can admire the craftsmen and their wheel moulding the lump of clay into a graceful receptacle. Their skilful gestures betray an inherited artistic ability. Guellala

Exhibits in the folk arts and traditions museum.

Typical views of the countryside of Djerba.

is especially charming in the late afternoon, when the sun sinks gloriously into the sea.

Houmt Souk is the administrative, financial and trade centre of the island. Its souks bustle with activity, and craft objects, especially materials, woollen blankets and copper objects are on sale, while weavers work their looms. Djerba was famous for its jewellery, and several workshops, run by Jewish goldsmiths, excelled in the making of traditional jewels, filigree, enamelled pieces, often embellished with beautifully coloured stones. This craft, is however, in the process of disappearing.

The arts and folk traditions museum is to be found within the beautiful building, the Zawiya of Sidi Zitoumi. The museum is educational, and provides a wealth of information on the different traditional aspects of the island. Exhibits include a rich collection of costumes of the various ethnic groups and for special circumstances (Arab, Berber, Jewish-Berber, weddings, etc.), a beautiful collection of Koramic texts and Koran boxes, and an infinitely varied jewel collection reflecting the skills of the Djerbian goldsmiths of the past. A room of the museum has been reconstructed into a potter's workshop, while another annex contains a reconstruction of a weaving workshop. Also on show is a large collection of pottery, including a range of everyday utensils peculiar to the island, and a collection of carved furniture.

Fisherman near El Kantara.

Views of the beach.

Contents

INTRODUCTION	2	THE CENTRAL-WESTERN REGION	52
THE PREHISTORIC PERIOD	3	ZAGHOUAN	53
THE PUNIC PERIOD	4	THUBURBO MAJUS	54
THE MASSYLE KINGDOM	6	DOUGGA	56
THE ROMAN PERIOD	6	MAKTAR	60
THE VANDAL AND BYZANTINE PERIOD	8	TESTOUR	62
THE ISLAMIC FATH (THE BIRTH OF ISLAM)	9	LE KEF	63
		THE CAP-BON REGION	64
THE ORIGINS OF THE REIGNING DYNASTIES	10	HAMMAMET	65
		NABEUL	68
THE AGHLABID PERIOD	10	KERKOUANE	72
THE FATIMID PERIOD	10	THE SAHEL	76
THE ZIRID PERIOD	11	THE ISLAMIC MUSEUM OF RAQQADA	77
THE HAFSID PERIOD	11	KAIROUAN	79
THE TURKISH PERIOD	11	SOUSSE	84
THE HUSSEINITE PERIOD	12	PORT EL KATAOUI	90
THE PROTECTORATE	12	MONASTIR	92
COMBATANT TUNISIA	13	MAHDIA	94
INDEPENDENCE	13	EL DJEM	96
THE MEDINA OF TUNIS	14	SFAX	98
THE DAR BEN ABDALLAH MUSEUM	16	SOUTHERN TUNISIA	101
THE NEW CITY	22	SBEITLA (SUFETULA)	102
BARDO MUSEUM	23	GAFSA	103
THE NORTHERN SUBURBS OF TUNIS	32	TOZEUR	104
CARTHAGE	33	NEFTA	105
SIDI BOU SAID	36	GABES	108
THE NORTH-EASTERN REGION	38	THE LAND OF MATMATA	110
UTICA	39	CHENINI	112
BIZERTE	40	THE KSOURS OF MEDENINE	113
THE NORTH-WESTERN REGION	44	ZARZIS	114
CHEMTOU	45	GIGHTIS	116
BULLA REGIA	46	DJERBA	117
TABARKA	48		

Acknowledgments:

Our thanks are due: to the Ministry of Cultural Affairs, National Institute of Archaeology and Art for permission to take photographs of antiquities and other art objects; to the Ministry of Tourism and other Government departments for their assistance in the preparation of this edition; to Mrs Jacqueline Karageorgis for editing the French texts of this edition and Mrs Gloria Joannides, Miss Bouli Hadjioannou and Mr Belazreg Nejib for preparing the English translation of this edition; to Mr Andreas Coutas for taking most of the photographs exclusively commissioned for this edition; to the administration and staff of the mosques, museums and archaeological sites for their assistance with the photography; special thanks are due to Mr Rached Fourati.

Collection ALL EUROPE

#	Title	Spanish	French	English	German	Italian	Catalan	Dutch	Swedish	Portuguese	Japanese	Finnish
1	ANDORRA	●	●	●	●	●	●					
2	LISBON	●	●	●	●	●				●		
3	LONDON	●	●	●	●	●					●	
4	BRUGES	●	●	●	●			●				
5	PARIS	●	●	●	●	●				●		
6	MONACO	●	●	●	●	●						
7	VIENNA	●	●	●	●	●			●	●		
8	NICE	●	●	●	●							
9	CANNES	●	●	●	●							
10	ROUSSILLON	●	●	●	●		●					
11	VERDUN	●	●	●	●							
12	THE TOWER OF LONDON	●	●	●	●							
13	ANTWERP	●	●	●	●			●				
14	WESTMINSTER ABBEY	●	●	●	●							
15	THE SPANISH RIDING SCHOOL IN VIENNA	●	●	●	●	●						
16	FATIMA	●	●	●	●	●			●			
17	WINDSOR CASTLE	●	●	●	●	●				●		
18	THE OPAL COAST		●	●								
19	COTE D'AZUR	●	●	●	●	●						
20	AUSTRIA		●	●	●							
21	LOURDES	●	●	●	●							
22	BRUSSELS	●	●	●	●			●				
23	SCHÖNBRUNN PALACE	●	●	●	●	●			●			
24	ROUTE OF PORT WINE	●	●	●	●					●		
25	CYPRUS		●	●	●				●			
26	HOFBURG PALACE	●	●	●	●							
27	ALSACE		●	●	●							
28	RHODES		●	●	●							
29	BERLIN		●	●	●							
30	CORFU		●	●	●							
31	MALTA		●	●	●							
32	PERPIGNAN		●									
33	STRASBOURG	●	●	●	●							
34	MADEIRA	●	●	●	●							
35	CERDAGNE · CAPCIR		●				●					

Collection ART IN SPAIN

#	Title	Spanish	French	English	German	Italian	Catalan	Dutch	Swedish	Portuguese	Japanese	Finnish
1	PALAU DE LA MUSICA CATALANA (Catalan Palace of Music)	●	●	●	●		●					
2	GAUDI	●	●	●	●	●					●	
3	PRADO MUSEUM I (Spanish Painting)	●	●	●	●	●					●	
4	PRADO MUSEUM II (Foreign Painting)	●	●	●	●	●						
5	MONASTERY OF GUADALUPE	●										
6	THE CASTLE OF XAVIER	●	●	●	●						●	
7	THE FINE ARTS MUSEUM OF SEVILLE	●	●	●	●							
8	SPANISH CASTLES	●	●	●	●							
9	THE CATHEDRALS OF SPAIN	●	●	●	●							
10	THE CATHEDRAL OF GERONA	●	●	●	●							
11	GRAN TEATRE DEL LICEU DE BARCELONA (The Great Opera House)	●	●	●	●	●	●					
12	THE ROMANESQUE STYLE IN CATALONIA	●	●	●	●							
13	LA RIOJA: ART TREASURES AND WINE-GROWING RESOURCES	●	●	●	●							
14	PICASSO	●	●	●	●							
15	REALES ALCAZARES (ROYAL PALACE OF SEVILLE)	●	●	●	●	●						
16	MADRID'S ROYAL PALACE	●	●	●	●	●						
17	ROYAL MONASTERY OF EL ESCORIAL	●	●	●	●	●						
18	THE WINES OF CATALONIA	●										
19	THE ALHAMBRA AND THE GENERALIFE	●	●	●	●							
20	GRANADA AND THE ALHAMBRA (ARAB AND MAURESQUE MONUMENTS OF CORDOVA, SEVILLE AND GRANADA)	●										
21	ROYAL ESTATE OF ARANJUEZ	●	●	●	●	●						
22	ROYAL ESTATE OF EL PARDO	●	●	●	●	●						
23	ROYAL HOUSES	●	●	●	●	●						
24	ROYAL PALACE OF SAN ILDEFONSO	●	●	●	●	●						
25	HOLY CROSS OF THE VALLE DE LOS CAIDOS	●	●	●	●	●						
26	OUR LADY OF THE PILLAR OF SARAGOSSA	●	●	●			●					

Collection ALL SPAIN

#	Title	Spanish	French	English	German	Italian	Catalan	Dutch	Swedish	Portuguese	Japanese	Finnish
1	ALL MADRID	●	●	●	●	●					●	
2	ALL BARCELONA	●	●	●	●	●	●					
3	ALL SEVILLE	●	●	●	●	●					●	
4	ALL MAJORCA	●	●	●	●	●		●				
5	ALL THE COSTA BRAVA	●	●	●	●	●						
6	ALL MALAGA and the Costa del Sol	●	●	●	●	●			●			
7	ALL THE CANARY ISLANDS, Gran Canaria, Lanzarote and Fuerteventura	●	●	●	●	●		●	●			
8	ALL CORDOBA	●	●	●	●	●					●	
9	ALL GRANADA	●	●	●	●	●						
10	ALL VALENCIA	●	●	●	●	●					●	
11	ALL TOLEDO	●	●	●	●	●						
12	ALL SANTIAGO	●	●	●	●	●						
13	ALL IBIZA and Formentera	●	●	●	●	●						
14	ALL CADIZ and the Costa de la Luz	●	●	●	●	●						
15	ALL MONTSERRAT	●	●	●	●							
16	ALL SANTANDER and Cantabria	●	●	●	●							
17	ALL THE CANARY ISLANDS II, Tenerife, La Palma, Gomera, Hierro	●	●	●	●	●		●	●			●
18	ALL ZAMORA	●	●	●	●							
19	ALL PALENCIA	●	●	●	●							
20	ALL BURGOS, Covarrubias and Santo Domingo de Silos	●	●	●	●	●						
21	ALL ALICANTE and the Costa Blanca	●	●	●	●	●			●			
22	ALL NAVARRA	●	●	●	●							
23	ALL LERIDA, Province and Pyrenees	●	●	●	●				●			
24	ALL SEGOVIA and Province	●	●	●	●							
25	ALL SARAGOSSA and Province	●	●	●	●	●						
26	ALL SALAMANCA and Province	●	●	●	●	●		●				
27	ALL AVILA and Province	●	●	●	●							
28	ALL MINORCA	●	●	●	●							
29	ALL SAN SEBASTIAN and Guipúzcoa	●	●	●	●							
30	ALL ASTURIAS	●	●	●	●							
31	ALL LA CORUNA and the Rías Altas	●	●	●	●							
32	ALL TARRAGONA and Province	●	●	●	●							
33	ALL MURCIA and Province	●	●	●	●							
34	ALL VALLADOLID and Province	●	●	●	●							
35	ALL GIRONA and Province	●	●									
36	ALL HUESCA and Province	●	●									
37	ALL JAEN and Province	●	●	●	●							
38	ALL ALMERIA and Province	●	●	●	●							
39	ALL CASTELLON and the Costa del Azahar	●	●	●	●							
40	ALL CUENCA and Province	●	●	●	●							
41	ALL LEON and Province	●	●	●	●							
42	ALL PONTEVEDRA, VIGO and the Rías Bajas	●	●	●	●							
43	ALL RONDA	●	●	●	●	●						
44	ALL SORIA	●		●								
45	ALL HUELVA	●	●	●	●							
46	ALL EXTREMADURA	●										
47	ALL GALICIA	●	●	●	●	●						
48	ALL ANDALUSIA	●	●	●	●							
49	ALL CATALONIA	●	●	●	●	●	●	●				
50	ALL LA RIOJA	●	●	●	●							

Collection ALL AMERICA

#	Title	Spanish	French	English	German	Italian	Catalan	Dutch	Swedish	Portuguese	Japanese	Finnish
1	PUERTO RICO	●		●								
2	SANTO DOMINGO	●										
3	QUEBEC			●								
4	COSTA RICA	●		●								

Collection ALL AFRICA

#	Title	Spanish	French	English	German	Italian	Catalan	Dutch	Swedish	Portuguese	Japanese	Finnish
1	MOROCCO	●	●	●	●	●						
2	THE SOUTH OF MOROCCO	●	●	●	●	●						
3	TUNISIA			●	●							

The printing of this book was completed in the workshops of
FISA - ESCUDO DE ORO, S.A.
Palaudarias, 26 · Barcelona (Spain)

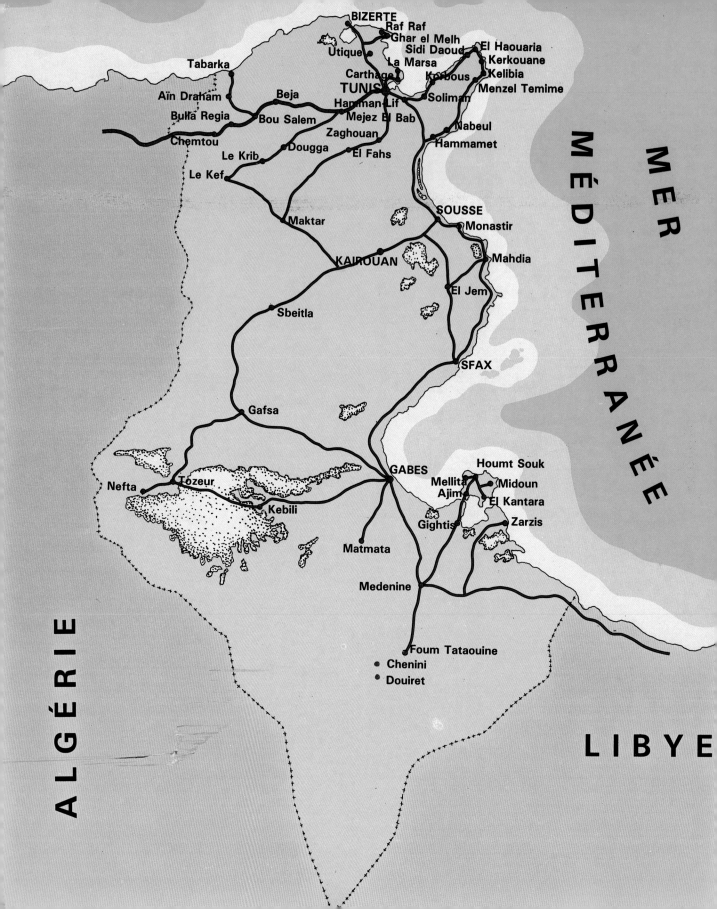